# FREE
## TO
### *Be*

# FREE
## TO
## *Be*

## A SIX WEEK GUIDE TO
## RECLAIMING YOUR SOUL

## SHIRIN ETESSAM

POST Hill
PRESS

A POST HILL PRESS BOOK
ISBN: 978-1-63758-546-7
ISBN (eBook): 978-1-63758-547-4

Free to Be:
A Six-Week Guide to Reclaiming Your Soul
© 2023 by Shirin Etessam
All Rights Reserved

Cover design by Hampton Lamoureux

Interior Design by Yoni Limor

Post Hill Press
New York • Nashville
posthillpress.com

Published in the United States of America
1 2 3 4 5 6 7 8 9 10

To my magnificent father, Iraj Etessam, who passed away just as this book was going to print and to my incredible ever-present mother, Iran Etessam. Together, you've taught me the value of commitment, the meaning of love, and the importance of family. Individually, you've taught me to find meaning in my work, to approach the world with grace and integrity and have given me the biggest gift of all—the freedom to be. This book is dedicated to you with all the love in the universe.

# Table of Contents

## Part One

*Part Two*

"Your beliefs become your thoughts,
Your thoughts become your words,
Your words become your actions,
Your actions become your habits,
Your habits become your values,
Your values become your destiny."

**—Gandhi**

# Introduction

## Realizing What's Possible, After Facing the Seemingly Impossible

Imagine you wander into a thrift store on a lazy Sunday afternoon. As you meander around aimlessly looking for a hidden treasure of sorts, you spot a little statue. You dust it off, look at it in the light, and it reminds you of your childhood. You feel there's some inner magical pull toward it. Fixated, you buy it for five dollars and put it on your dresser.

Over time, your friends and family comment on what a cool find it is. On a whim, you decide to get it appraised, and much to your and the appraiser's astonishment and delight, the statue belonged to a substantial and significant collection but had gone missing. Your five-dollar figure is invaluable—worth more than five million dollars!

Now, what if I told you that statue or treasure is your soul? A soul that the external blows of life have repeatedly pushed down, diminished, buried, and weighed down. Life has pushed your soul to the corner—and it's just been sitting there, neglected, and gathering dust. All the while, you are living the life you believe others expect you to live. To no avail, though. Your stifled soul creates tension, snuffs your creativity, and smothers the light you were born to bring to others.

Scientists estimate that the observable universe's diameter is about ninety-three billion light-years, and it contains two trillion galaxies. It would take about forty-six billion light-years to travel between the Earth and the edge of the observable universe. As a reminder, a light-year is about six trillion miles. Not one galaxy is the same, not one star, not one planet, not one organism.

In other words, you are incredibly, uniquely you. Yet, we are raised and taught to be, act, speak, and think like others. And the unique star that was born and shined majestically in its early years begins to dim its light and acclimates to the dullness we call life.

This book isn't about how to change your life. It is not a how-to or a traditional self-help book. It is not a manual on how to become more productive or to be more organized.

This book is about excavating your soul from the massive jumble called "life" to connect with it on a deeper level, honor it, nurture it, play with it, and eventually set it free. Ultimately, this book is about how to allow your soul to pave your new way. If this sounds too "woo woo" for you, you may be surprised to hear that I was once like you. Please allow me to explain.

My soul journey started in late 2013 after a breakup with my partner of thirteen years. She was a dear friend for nine years before our relationship. Twenty-two years of love, friendship, and partnership vanished after a twenty-minute conversation. This breakup solidified the end of a bond I once thought was eternal.

In the days, weeks, months, and years to follow, I learned more about the part I played in our relationship's demise, which I will share throughout this book. But in those early hours, days, and weeks, I felt like I was in an abyss of nothingness.

As I lay there the first night after the conversation, I knew everything was about to change, and I had no clue, and I genuinely mean sub-zero knowledge of what would come next. I simply had no Plan B, and I was petrified of what the separation would do to our kids, who were five and seven at the time.

As angry, upset, and confused as I was then, I knew that I had work to do, which was ultimately my responsibility. I had an ultimatum of either making a massive shift or continue going down the same path, spiraling deeper into the dark hole.

Or I could shield myself and the kids from experiencing another blow to our lives. The big disappointment of the separation was terrible enough; I would not let my complete undoing wreck our lives further. I simply wasn't going to let it happen.

Staring at the ceiling that fateful night, I knew the pain I was feeling, which was truly unbearable, wasn't just about my broken heart—everything was broken.

Throughout the years, before the breakup, I was drifting further away from who I wanted and needed to become. My identity, and more importantly my magic, had diminished. I was ungrounded and vulnerable. I now call that time "my walking dead years." How dead you may ask? Well, so bad that my coworkers staged an intervention. No kidding. I was on the executive team of a startup, and about a year or so after I started, our

CEO flew the executive team to St. Petersburg, Florida for an important meeting. We had much fun on that trip, but one night, my dear coworkers (who have now become close friends) called me into their room, and much to my surprise, they had an "intervention" with me. They sat me down, poured a glass of wine, and told me I *had to* get out of my relationship and that I was being boiled alive, slowly but surely. This was at least a year and a half, if not two, before the breakup. What did I do? Nothing!

As I laid there the night of the breakup, it became apparent that the way I was thinking was not serving me, and my body was always exhausted from lack of sleep and being "on" all the time.

I was the slow boiling frog[1] for at least a good five years before the breakup. Heat rising to a very full boil... and I didn't move. I didn't even plan to move! Why?

There are many reasons, which I will share throughout this book, but the short answer is I forgot my magic. I was so concentrated on my partner, the kids, and the life I thought we were supposed to have that I spent very little time on myself—which I know is far too common.

And in full transparency, I viewed people working on themselves as indulgent and selfish. Where they found the time and space to do so was beyond me. I was just grateful to get through the day without collapsing. I also didn't give a poop about being more productive or better organized or the ten steps to a healthier life...or whatever other answers "self-help" books provided. I felt broken... incomplete...MIA while I was being incredibly productive, super organized, and eating healthy. What I didn't know

---

1    *Farlex Dictionary of Idioms.* S.v. "boiling frog." Retrieved November 15, 2022 from https://idioms.thefreedictionary.com/boiling+frog.

was that my soul, wherever it was hidden, was begging for something *much* deeper!

For me, there is no specific God, but I do believe there are powers, frequencies, energies far beyond our comprehension that are constantly at work. This belief is why I'm endlessly fascinated with physics, cosmology, and neuroplasticity—where science and spirituality dance together in all sorts of magical patterns. I also believe in a God within. For me, it is the true definition of the soul.

Until the breakup, I was what I call a half-ass spiritualist. Calling on God and the powers that be whenever I was in trouble and making deals like, "If you get me out of this mess, I promise to believe in you, etc." I would also visit spirituality here and there by going on weekend retreats, meditating whenever convenient, exploring spiritual centers such as Spirit Rock (now one of my top happy places), etc. Still, the visits were always random and only when convenient. I didn't make it a central part of my life. I didn't feed my soul.

I learned quite early in my process that being a half-ass spiritualist doesn't work. You're either all in, or you're not at all. You either believe there is a Higher Power within and all around us. Or you don't. This journey is about that exploration of your soul and its connection to the universe.

Personally, it would have been impossible for me to do this work without believing in a Higher Power. But you can get something out of this book whether you believe in God or anything else that resonates with you—awareness, love, energy, Jesus, Buddha, Allah, etc. If you choose not to begin exploring a Higher Power, that is perfectly fine, but I imagine this book will feel like one of my random visits to spirituality—a spiritual window shopping of sorts. You will possibly see the benefits but not fully experience them. My wish for you is that you dive deep into what's possible, and the only way to do that is to trust what you can't see yet.

If you choose to join me on this journey for the next six weeks, please know there are no prerequisites—you can come as you are, wherever you are. In the early days, my mantra was simply "Better than this." I knew I could get to a better place. I think this is sadly common. You may be in that place now. You may be wondering how you will ever change your life. Your journey can start by committing to finding your authentic, full self.

To be clear, my life was not horrible before and not always perfect. I continue to make mistakes (because I am human), but from a very different space, and that space is everything.

For the first time in my life, I'm in love with who I am. I used to believe magic was elsewhere and with other people, especially with my ex. I truly thought she had the magic sauce and my life without her wouldn't be magical. I've come to realize how absolutely untrue (and unhealthy) that was. Today, I'm in the best relationship of my life. I love and adore my partnership with my wife. I have a wonderful relationship with my kids. I meditate regularly, sleep well, surround myself with only those I want to have in my life, and I don't take on projects that don't feed my soul.

It isn't roses and rainbows every day, but I am grateful for every single day (even those that suck), and I am much more aware of myself—when I've been hurt, when I need to pause, when I need to speak—and all the experiences that come with living from one's soul.

It took me half a dozen years to (re)discover my magic, gain the clarity I was desperately seeking, and create a life I am absolutely in love with. In my seeking, I left no stone unturned and looked in every nook and cranny of my being.

Though on my knees, lost and grieving, there was a richness, a realness I had not felt before. It was like the beautiful flowers were blooming from the darkest, deadest of roots. I was flourishing by finding myself. Instead of ignoring those deep, dark, damp, and often frightening places we fear to visit, I walked straight into them, spent time there, moved things around, weeded some out, and planted new seeds.

At the time, it just looked like manure, worms, and last year's compost that I was wading in. I didn't realize then that I was sowing what I would reap in the next seasons. And it would be a bountiful harvest.

I've spent the last few years distilling what I've discovered and realized that my process in the previous six years could truly be done in six weeks, if only I had known what to do. In a way, I wish there had been a book like this when I was going through my transformation process ("bobbing for spiritual apples," as I like to call it). I want to spare you some (maybe, hopefully, most) of that pain and confusion in this book. An intentional life only comes from living intentionally. It's not something you can do in your spare time or here and there. You have to embrace it and hit the ground running wholeheartedly.

That's not to say you won't be working your butt off to become the new, beautiful you. There will be blood, sweat, and tears (okay, maybe not blood), but sweat and tears most certainly. My wish is that most of the work will strengthen you, and most of the tears (if not all) will be happy. My sincerest hope is that this work will move you. My goal in writing this book is to help you rework your life into a life you love. Sadly, so many people who have exceptional qualities to share with the world instead waste so much precious time. I was one of these until I found the connection between my soul, mind, body, and heart that freed me from a life half-lived.

Professionally, I've done extensive work in the world of media. The question was: could I write a book on transformation? That, dear reader, remains to be seen. All I can do is share what I've discovered, and I hope this book resonates with others who find themselves where I was. Through these next pages and chapters, I want to take your hand, lead you to the lost treasure, help you dust it off, take it home, learn the real value (and potency) of it, and have this find become the most profound shift in your life.

> "Who looks outside, dreams. Who looks inside, awakes."
>
> **—Carl Jung**

This book is my sincere attempt to share an incredible process with you, and what took me six painstaking years to figure out, so you can transform into your authentic, awesome self in just six weeks. You're welcome! ;)

# How to Get the Most Out of This Book

This book is written in two parts, with each part representing a period of twenty-one days—three weeks—in which you will be making significant changes in your life. The first three weeks (twenty-one days) are intended to break habits that do not serve you, and the second three weeks (twenty-one days) are structured to create lasting soul-driven habits that will shift and shape your life, profoundly. The journey begins with a commitment to engaging in the text and exploring the exercises included. These are not necessary tasks.

Instead of being a coach who will demand things you are not comfortable doing or simply don't want to do, I will be a guide to your spirit so that we can take a magical mystery tour toward an existence that is full. You may feel awkward at times, but this uneasiness is like turning a corner, only to find miracles awaiting.

The magical path you once only sensed was there but never traversed is your trail toward your new, exciting life, unfolding.

# PART 1

The first three weeks are about clearing the way for your soul to be discovered, buried beneath the weight of this life. We begin the journey by clearing your mind, heart, and body. Out of the three, the mind is the most unruly and dictates the rest. So that's where we begin.

Once you've refreshed your mind, we move to the heart and body. These also need tending and resetting. The final result is the trinity within you (heart, body, and mind) will be welcoming of your soul, creating a holy quaternity (mind, body, heart, and soul) that is the re-visioned you.

As you progress through this section, give this book to yourself like a treat. A sanctuary. Something to take refuge in. If you're not used to "me time" this would be a good time to tell your loved ones that you're practicing self-care.

# PART 2

The second part of the book is about granting your soul permission to lead, once you have connected with it, and know what a life-saving device it can be. Whispering from your brain to your heart and body are soul winks that will guide your way. Setting your soul free breaks through all the noise of this life, silences fears, and welcomes you to a life that you want and never knew you needed so much. For your soul to be set free and lead your life, you need not just appreciate your soul but become realigned with it.

By Week 6, with a clear mindset, a comforted heart, a nourished body, a rediscovered (playful) soul, and a relationship with your Higher Power, you will begin living a new ethos. Refreshed, you will emerge with a promise that this new re-visioned story will become your manifesto.

## NOTE ON THE EXERCISES

I have designed the exercises in this book in a very doable way to be integrated seamlessly within your busy workday or day off. You won't need to sit on top of a picturesque mountaintop in isolation to reap the benefits of this book.

To achieve anything mentioned here, you need only to read the content and interact with it in the here and now, exactly where you are and at any point throughout the day. Though the exercises are not mandatory, if you are going to choose just one set of exercises to do, I highly recommend the Daily Morning Purges, as these activities bring you the best lasting results.

In addition to the Daily Morning Purges, there are daily exercises at the end of each chapter. How you choose to experience this book is entirely up to you because it's your journey. I would suggest that if you are a fast reader, to read a full chapter on your first day of each week and then do the daily exercises for the week each day, then read the next chapter on the first day of the following week and do the daily exercises for that week and so on. The exercises are very snackable and can be completed in less than ten minutes a day. If you are a slow reader, please read at your pace but be sure to do an exercise a day. By doing so, your process becomes experiential and not just conceptual. It's the difference between "Oh, that's a nifty idea" and "OMG, I haven't felt this alive in years!"

However you choose to experience this book, my request is that you do so chronologically, as its structure from one week to the next is very intentional.

With that said, shall we begin?

# Part One

# Week 1
## Brain Detox

### THE PROBLEMS ARE ALL IN OUR HEAD: WE ARE ON AUTOPILOT

Have you ever gotten into your car, driven somewhere, arrived, and could not recall how you got there because you were so lost in your thoughts while driving? I can't tell you how many times I've driven over the Golden Gate Bridge and couldn't recall doing so. The Golden Gate Bridge, one of the wonders of the world...and I am way too busy in my head! Insert eyeroll and cringe.

A scientific study conducted by Harvard psychologists Matthew A. Killingsworth and Daniel T. Gilbert revealed that adults spend at least half of their day thinking about something other than what they are doing at any given moment. Living a life busy with an endless list of to-dos, the regrets of yesterday, and worries about tomorrow that we rarely get a glimpse of the here and now. As we continue on autopilot from one year to the next, to the next, to the next...one day we wake up and wonder why we're not happy.

Meandering thoughts lead to a meandering life. Intentional thoughts, intentional life.

I was completely on autopilot during my walking dead years. So much so that I didn't know how to operate in any other way. I remember one day my ex suggested I take the day off of work and offered to take care of the kids. While I was surprised and delighted by the generous and rare offer, I had no clue what to do with myself. I ended up wandering around my hometown and then another town, aimlessly. I felt like such a loser. A whole day to myself and I couldn't think of a way to take care of myself? This should have been a huge clue that I had been living life on autopilot! But nope, I was just glad to get back to my routine instead of really questioning why I had such a hard time taking one day to take care of myself.

For some, being on autopilot shows up in the careers they find themselves in. Some polls show that nearly 85 percent of professionals lack engagement when at work, ultimately suggesting that they are unhappy doing what they do day in and day out.[2] According to the Harvard study, a wandering mind makes us unhappy. We find ourselves moving through life distracted, which diminishes our creativity.

There are of course a variety of reasons that contribute to our unhappiness, but I believe much of it is based on the fact that most of us have no clue why we're here—there is no raison d'être, a reason or purpose for living. For most seeking a new path, how you live externally simply hasn't

2    Clarisse, "Why 85% of People Hate their Jobs," Staff Squared, December 3, 2019, https://www.staffsquared.com/blog/why-85-of-people-hate-their-jobs/#:~:text=A%20global%20poll%20conducted%20by,are%20unhappy%20in%20their%20jobs.

matched what you feel internally—yet. This is why being intentional about what you focus on, think about, and do is vital when deciding to detox your brain.

## THE CONTENT WE CONSUME

> "You become what you digest into your spirit. Whatever you think about, focus on, read about, talk about, you're going to attract more of into your life. Make sure they're all positive."
>
> **—Germany Kent**

They say content is king. I can't argue with that, because that's what I do as a vocation: I produce content to be consumed. The work I create tells stories, and the audience is pulled into those stories. At the core of content is a real, beating heart. It's the story that the person is telling the world. But not all content is the same. If you are choosing to mindlessly consume content and not considering whether or not the content is serving you, the ramifications can be similar to eating whatever, whenever you want.

Think about it this way. If you don't pay attention to what you eat, you will eat mindlessly. On the other hand, if you are aware of what you consume, you can reap incredible health benefits. Making it a priority to eat meals that not only nourish your body but your soul is life-changing.

The same is true of becoming more conscious of what content you consume and striving to ensure that the content elevates your mood, enhances your learning, and overall feeds your soul.

Alternatively, if you endlessly consume mental junk food, you can feel depressed, disillusioned, and uninspired. This can come in the form of violent movies, reality shows, salacious magazines...and even the news. How many of you wake up and turn on the morning news as part of your morning routine? While I believe staying abreast of global, national and local news is important, you don't need it packaged and fed to you every day, especially first thing in the morning.

Consuming content that doesn't serve you can poison your thoughts and make your reality not what it can and should be. Consuming content that aligns with your well-being can enhance your life and elevate it to a higher level of positivity.

## UNDERSTANDING CONTENT OVERLOAD

What is the first thing you do after you post a story, image, or video to social media? You check back to see how many "likes" it has. We all do it. This is why and how social media works. The dopamine levels in the brain increase, so we want more. This same chemical reaction that scientists have proven is similar to that of individuals who suffer from addiction lights our brains up like holiday decor. As notifications light up on our screens, we keep coming back for more—endlessly.

As a tool, content delivered through TV, radio, computers, IOT (the internet of things), handheld devices, and the like can synergize us and allow us to get things done at warp speed. But, as an unchecked force running rampant in our lives, it can empty us of our spark.

So why are there so many of us scrolling continuously on social media, endlessly answering emails, and sleeping our lives away instead of supercharging our creativity?

Television, news, the internet, and social media over time have arguably been bogged down with nonsense and negativity. But social media doesn't have to diminish your energy day in and day out. You can choose to divert your attention elsewhere.

The internet and social media can connect people to share great ideas, or it can inundate, overwhelm, and lead to "info-xication." The choice of what content you consume, and when, is yours.

Overstimulation and information overload (info-xication) can influence our ability to connect, because our mind's capacity is shrunk to where we can't fit much more. And we can become more accustomed to engaging through a screen than connecting with others in person, who mean the most to us. Our energy can be zapped with our inability to truly connect with others, and our true self... which can ultimately lead to a decline in our mental health.

A 2019 CDC Youth Risk Behavior Surveillance Data Sum-mary and Trends Report[3] highlighted a growing trend of mental health issues in high school students in the United States. More than one in three high school students had experienced persistent feelings of sadness

---

3  "Youth Risk Behavior Survey Data Summary & Trends Report 2009-2019," Centers for Disease Control and Prevention, accessed November 16, 2022, https://www.cdc.gov/healthyyouth/data/yrbs/pdf/YRBSDataSummaryTrendsReport2019-508.pdf.

or hopelessness in 2019, a 40 percent increase since 2009. In 2019, approximately one in six youth reported making a suicide plan in the past year, a 44 percent increase since 2009. This is the first generation growing up with social media. Coincidence? Experts don't think so. I don't either.

A documentary/drama film released in 2020 by Netflix, *The Social Dilemma*, explored this dynamic dichotomy; the technology that was developed to be a tool to connect us also has the capacity to divide us, make us question our self-worth, and isolate us. Even the tech gurus who created social networking are now forewarning about negative impacts.[4]

Clinical psychologist Dr. Amelia Aldao shared on NPR in 2020 that "doomscrolling" puts minds into a "vicious cycle of negativity."[5] Similar to what the docudrama demonstrates, this constant loop of doomsday thoughts rewires our minds. We do, however, have the power to unlock the spell by deciding what content we consume, when we consume it, and for how long. But as a global community we felt like we had less of a choice when COVID-19 hit in early 2020.

During the pandemic, many had to quarantine, and one of the most common ways to connect was through social media. And since many were so busy before the global health crisis, when faced with schedules cleared of commitments, some chose to use streaming services and social media more than ever. Not surprisingly, the Centers

---

4   *The Social Dilemma*, directed by Jeff Orlowski (Exposure Labs, 2020), https://www.thesocialdilemma.com/.

5   Lulu Garcia-Navarro, "Your 'Doomscrolling' Breeds Anxiety. Here's How To Stop The Cycle," *Weekend Edition Sunday*, NPR, July 19, 2020, https://www.npr.org/2020/07/19/892728595/your-doomscrolling-breeds-anxiety-here-s-how-to-stop-the-cycle.

for Disease Control began noticing trends of depression, suicidal ideation, substance abuse, domestic abuse, and loneliness increasing dramatically too.[6]

This is not just a warning about content overload. It's all about mind control—on the individual and collective level. The creators of social media platforms admit in the docudrama that they didn't intend for their creations to become a Frankenstein that can manipulate the masses.[7]

Social media was not intended to consume us instead of us consuming it. Still, the more "intelligent" the platforms and apps (AI) become, the more they feed us what they think we want to know, hear, and see.

So, for example, if you thought something specific about any of the social justice issues of 2020 being lobbied by 2020 presidential candidates—Black Lives Matter, global warming, COVID-19, healthcare, voting rights—social media (and the news channel you chose to watch) fed you more info to reinforce that. The country was more polarized than ever during the year of 2020 because, with quarantine in full force, people were primarily connected through those platforms. Thus, many lost their true connection to their true self and sincere connections that happen in real life.

This is not meant to be a PSA where I declare that deleting all social media, deciding to consume more

---

6    Mark E. Czeisler et al., "Mental Health, Substance Use, and Suicidal Ideation During the COVID-19 Pandemic — United States, June 24-30, 2020," Centers for Disease Control and Prevention, *Morbidity and Mortality Weekly Report*, Vol. 69, No. 32 (August 14, 2020), https://www.cdc.gov/mmwr/volumes/69/wr/pdfs/mm6932a1-H.pdf.

7    Devika Girish, "'The Social Dilemma' Review: Unplug and Run," *The New York Times*, September 9, 2020, https://www.nytimes.com/2020/09/09/movies/the-social-dilemma-review.html.

uplifting media, and replacing those activities with x, y, or z will solve all of your life's problems. I am simply saying that many years after the first social networking sites launched, as a society, we now collectively can suffer from content overload if we're not careful. And this phenomenon has the potential to distract us, drain us, and overall stifle our creativity.

## RECOVERING FROM INFO-XICATION

"We are drowning in information while starving for wisdom."

—E.O. Wilson

The global average daily time spent consuming content is roughly seven hours, including phone, TV, and other digital media forms. Some of it is the information we need, but much of it is sheer mental junk food. The average person is awake for about fifteen hours. That means that nearly half of every waking hour, we are consuming content. That's half of your life!

This is true now more than ever. As we drown in "content" from the time we wake up to the time we go to sleep, there is little time to do anything unless you schedule it in or set boundaries.

Info-xication (also known as infobesity, information overload, information anxiety, and information explosion) is the difficulty in understanding an issue and effectively making decisions when one has too much information about that issue. It is generally associated with the excessive quantity of daily information.

Content is not just in the form of television, movies, social media, radio, magazines, and newspapers, but the information we hear from our teachers, bosses, family, and friends. The issue is that, at times, we've inadvertently allowed the outer world's content to overshadow us. Then, before we know it, instead of developing our own story, we invite influences to do it for us. Most of us believe in what society has taught us, what they told us, what we witnessed, far before we believe in ourselves. And that is exactly how we became lost.

Recovering from info-xication means becoming the director of your mind, soul, heart, and body. This happens when you allow your soul to be your wayfinder. That's hard to do when your brain is overwhelmed with unneeded information not pertaining to your passions.

In my friend Tiffany Shlain's book, *24/6: Giving up Screens One Day a Week to Get More Time, Creativity, and Connection*, she recommends setting healthy boundaries and creating new digital habits that allow us to control what we receive and when.[8] The idea is that we should become very intentional about the content we consume, when we consume content, and when we shut it off to focus on what is most important to us. Even putting down our phones and devices one day a week can do wonders for our brains, bodies, and souls.

---

8    Tiffany Shlain, "24/6: Giving Up Screens One Day a Week to Get More Time, Creativity, and Connection," Goodreads (October 20, 2020) https://www.goodreads.com/en/book/show/55664309-24-6.

# DON'T BELIEVE EVERYTHING YOU THINK

> "Don't believe everything you think. Thoughts are just that—thoughts."
>
> **—Allan Lokos**

I used to wake up in the middle of the night in a complete panic. I was a total insomniac. For fifteen years I slept for three or four hours a night, which exacerbated the situation. The only way I could get out of my middle-of-the-night panic was to start working, so I would do some of my best work between 2 and 5 a.m. But I would start my day completely exhausted and cranky, and I wasn't the best mom or partner because of it.

One of the things I noticed about these panic attacks was that I would completely believe whatever I was thinking at that moment. My brain would tell me: *We are going to be penniless; I'm going to be found out (classic imposter syndrome); something is going to happen to my kids*; and so on. At the time I didn't realize these thoughts weren't real. I surmised, if I was thinking about them then they must be real. I would work myself into a complete panic (all while lying next to my partner in the middle of the night) and then try to ignore and suppress these thoughts in an attempt to make them go away. That led only to guilt for ignoring my so-called "problems," even though the problems were completely made up. And the problems compounded.

Humans tend to think every thought that comes into their minds is real. It isn't. And that's fortunate because many minds tend to conjure up negative thoughts.

According to the US National Science Foundation, an average person has about 12,000 to 60,000 thoughts per day. Of those, 80 percent are harmful, and **95 percent** are repetitive thoughts. Cognitive Behavioral Therapists have a term for it: ANTs (Automatic Negative Thoughts). Buddhists call it "the monkey mind." These thoughts include:

- **Fearful thoughts** that narrow your thinking and prevent you from taking action.

- **Stressful thoughts** that produce discomfort in the present moment.

- **Anxious thoughts** that create unpleasant feelings about the future.

Blame it on the Amygdala—I like to call her Amy G Dala. You've heard of the fight-or-flight response, right?[9] Well, that's Amy either duking it out in the ring or flying off to anywhere but here. Amy and I have had a looooong and sometimes tumultuous relationship because I have given her WAY too much power...until I realized I had a choice. You see, Amy can be a friend or foe depending on how you relate to her. Amy's main function is to sound the alarm for anything dangerous and to cause fear and anxiety. Some fears are merited, like the fear of getting hit

9    Mia Belle Frothingham, "Fight, Flight, Freeze, or Fawn: What This Response Means," SimplyPsycology, October 6, 2021, https://www.simplypsychology.org/fight-flight-freeze-fawn.html.

by a car or the fear of falling off a cliff. But she also causes undue anxiety over what she perceives as dangerous. Since our mind will believe anything we tell it repeatedly, if you believe in a thought, so will Amy, and she will do whatever necessary to protect you from the danger...even if it is completely made up and nonexistent. Given that 80 percent of our thoughts are harmful and negative, you can see where I am going with this—don't believe everything you think!

The truth is that thoughts are purely (passing) perceptions, not universal truths, and they come and go randomly. If we do not see thoughts for what they are—passing and often inaccurate perceptions—we will be a slave to them. Amy G Dala will win!

Emptying your mind begins with clearing negative thoughts that don't serve you, leaving newly cleared space for you to recognize and hear your own voice. By "clearing negative thoughts" I don't mean ignoring them or suppressing them (more about that in Week 5). By all means, invite them in, have them take a seat, see what they want. If it is nothing useful or beneficial, thank them for the visit and send them on their way. Thoughts will come regardless. We simply have no choice in the matter. What we can choose is whether to hold on to them or believe them. A "clearing" meditation (more on this soon) aids in this process.

There are many ways to quiet the mind. What Buddhists call "mindfulness" is ironically mindless-ness...or thoughtlessness (that is to free oneself from the barrage of constant thoughts), which, of course, is the most thoughtful thing you could ever do for yourself.

> "Rather than being your thoughts and emotions, be the awareness behind them."
>
> **—Eckhart Tolle**

Spiritual teacher and author Eckhart Tolle, in his book *The Power of Now*, said that our biggest barrier to experiencing a positive reality is discovered in our own minds.

Think about it. Everything we think, do, and say comes from our minds. We analyze and create within our brains. The adage "The mind is a dangerous place" is widely accepted as true, because it is. Our brains are powerful tools, with the power to destroy or create.

We either let our brains control us, or we manage our minds.

## WE ARE MEANING-MAKING MACHINES

> "Nothing is, unless our thinking makes it so."
>
> **—William Shakespeare**

The brain loves stories! It's how we categorize information. We observe situations, and our minds make up a story. It's how our brains make sense of the world. We tell ourselves stories about what we're observing, right or wrong.

We make everything mean something to us. When we perceive or experience something new that doesn't yet have meaning for us, we ascribe meaning to it. Nothing means anything, except for the meaning we assign it. In a nutshell, if we are the ones assigning meaning, then we can reassign or change meaning. We can tell ourselves a different story. We do that by emptying our minds first.

There is an old Zen story that is fitting here.

## Empty Your Cup

A university professor went to visit a famous Zen master. While the master quietly served tea, the professor talked about Zen. The master poured the visitor's cup to the brim, and then kept pouring. The professor watched the overflowing cup until he could no longer restrain himself. "It's full! No more will go in!" the professor blurted. "This is you," the master replied, "How can I show you Zen unless you first empty your cup?[10]

We have made clear that our minds are cluttered. So how do we declutter? Much like spring cleaning, we have to not only notice the clutter, but realize that less is more.

Emptying your mind doesn't mean you then stream thoughts that are meaningless. Or that you stop thinking entirely. It's quite the opposite. Once you have cleared your mind, you can assign more meaning to what you observe because your mind isn't as inundated. The more we correctly assign meaning to our thoughts, the more meaningful our lives become.

---

10   John Suler, "Zen Stories to Tell Your Neighbors," True Center Publishing, accessed November 22, 2022, https://truecenterpublishing.com/zenstory/emptycup.html.

# EMPTYING YOUR MIND TO MAKE ROOM FOR YOUR VOICE

So how do you empty your mind? Again, thoughts will come regardless. They truly don't stop. Try it right now. Try not to think. *"Stop."* I said, *"Stop thinking!!"* Isn't possible, is it? If you give up the idea that you can somehow block negative thoughts and stop beating yourself up for having them, you are halfway there.

The point is, thoughts come regardless, no matter who you are. There's a real art to being able to discern which ones are real and relevant and which ones are not. The space between you and your thoughts is where all your inner power—and inner peace—reside. If you can find that, it's magical.

One of the very best ways to create a separation from your thoughts is meditation, which we will dive into in Week 5. This week is all about choice: choosing to unplug as much as possible, to be very discerning about what content you read, watch, and hear, and to choose what you believe.

Remember, this is brain detox week. I am not asking you to unplug forever. I am suggesting a week of minimal information consumption. One must always be mindful of the information we absorb, but I recommend a week for this process.

The first time that I recall truly unplugging was when I visited Cuba for five weeks. Today, Cuba has internet cafes and parks, but back in 2000, there was nothing, and I mean nothing. There was no Wi-Fi and no cellular reception. No connection to the outside world. So, I truly had no choice but to unplug.

It was glorious! I could ground myself in the nature, culture, and people around me. I was with my best friend of many years, and it was during this trip that we fell in love. This was the beginning of me designing my story.

It was like stepping back in time. It felt as if I was a child again, carefree, and free to spend my time however I wanted. My soul was singing. We were "old schooling it" and we *loved* it. We were truly living.

We explored the country, spent days and nights listening to music, hung out with locals, and danced in the streets of Havana.

One particular night I was on the balcony of one of the singers of the Buena Vista Social Club singers (because Cuba is magical that way), and I was soaking it all in. The sounds, the smells, the sights. My heart was full.

Everyone and everything around me was very lively, and I was very aware of my surroundings. I was listening to music, watching and listening to a band busking below, and I was staring at and studying the crystal-clear starry sky.

I knew then and there that this is what it felt like to be fully alive in the moment, to be connected to other souls, and to be grateful for where you are, unencumbered by the past or future.

That moment and our entire stay in Cuba was sheer magic, and I have no doubt that a massive part of this magical experience unfolded because we were forced to unplug. And in doing so, were able to be fully present.

Of course, I realize an unplugged trip isn't practical for everyone, but you can steal away moments here and there within your day. Even as little as fifteen minutes away from your phone and computer can instill a sense of connection to the universe, and ground your whole existence.

By carving out time for yourself to be more mindful of what your mind and body are doing, you can take a pulse of your heart and soul. Failure to do so can mean you enter into autopilot mode where you're just going through the motions and dredging through life instead of designing the life you want, one that your whole being desperately needs.

I continue to practice unplugging as often as I can. I'm an entrepreneur, a parent, and a partner, and it can be difficult to accomplish this. I find, like many things in life, if I am intentional about unplugging, I will succeed in doing so.

When I unplug, I purposefully remove my phone and computer from my presence and become fully present in the moment.

When is the ideal time for you to unplug? For me, it's late in the afternoon and evenings, after work and my kids' schooling, on the weekends, and on holidays. For some, it may be easiest and best to do this in the quiet of the mornings. Exploring different times and techniques will help. And if necessary, physically remove the temptation. Place your devices elsewhere. Turn off notifications. And focus your time on the people, places, and experiences around you.

I admit it—it's not always easy, but it is very worthwhile.

# THOUGHTS CAN CONTROL YOU, OR YOU CAN CONTROL YOUR THOUGHTS

Thoughts in general—happy thoughts that serve you or doomsday thoughts that deplete you—have the potential to have the same power over your life. It's really the difference between awareness and thought. When you become aware that you are having thoughts, you can choose which thoughts to believe in and give energy to and what to let go of. So, you become aware that you are having thoughts rather than the thoughts having you.

Try this. The next time you have a thought, spend a little time with it, acknowledge you have the thought, and then let go. Then when another thought comes, do the same. And again, and again.

How do you let go of your thoughts? The answer is mindfulness. As soon as you let a thought go, return to the present moment, and then the release of another thought and bring your attention back to the present, and then again and again and again...and again. The more you can stay in the present, the more you can see the separation... the space between your awareness (in the present) and your thoughts.

Another way to let go is instead of reacting to everything you think, become an unbiased observer of your thoughts. Your reaction is the same from both stimuli. As much as possible, you have to be an unmoved scientist observing the experiments in your mind. Impulses go in, reactions ensue. Observations go as follows:

- When harmful thoughts arise, say, "It's interesting that I think that."

- When helpful thoughts arise, say, "It's interesting that I think that."

See a pattern in your (non)reaction here?

As an unbiased observer of your thoughts, you remain in control and non-reactionary. When you become the observer, you know that you have thoughts, rather than the thoughts having you.

This awareness is everything, as it will give you the ability to choose which thoughts to believe and concentrate on andwhich ones to let go of. As the Native American parable goes, the wolf you feed, whether positive or negative, is the one that wins.[11]

Michael Singer, the guru of minding your mind, said it another way:

> "There is nothing more important to true growth than realizing that you are not the voice of the mind—you are the one who hears it. If you don't understand this, you will try to figure out which of the many things the voice says is really you. People go through so many changes in the name of "trying to find myself." They want to discover which of these voices, which of these aspects of their personality, is who they really are. The answer is simple: none of them."
>
> **—Michael Singer, *The Untethered Soul***

---

11  Alyssa Yeo, LPC, CYT, "The Story of Two Wolves," Urban Balance, February 24, 2016, https://urbanbalance.com/the-story-of-two-wolves/.

# HOW CAN YOU SPEND YOUR TIME UNPLUGGED?

Listen to music, ideally with no vocals (jazz, classical, lounge, spa, etc.), go for walks, organize your room, clean the garage, hang out with family members and friends, dance, play board games like chess, backgammon, and scrabble. Puzzles are always a crowd pleaser! If that's a snooze fest for you, do what speaks to you. Or what used to tickle your fancy as a child or young adult.

It is difficult to truly unplug in today's world. I know it is! They say discipline is a muscle. I agree, but here's another anatomy analogy.

> "Once something moves from our brains to our bones, that's when we can use it to change our lives."
>
> **—Jen Sincero**

The next step is choosing to carve out this time for yourself.

You'll notice that your thoughts start getting louder and louder when you block information from coming in. You drown out the noise around you and tune into your inner self.

People who have gone to silent meditation retreats often say that their thoughts become more intense and incessant. So, what do you do with all the nasty little gremlins that come rushing in and take over? You let them in, acknowledge them, and then let them go. You don't feed them. Remember, gremlins only become gross little monsters when you feed them.

## CARVING OUT SPACE TO BE CREATIVE

> "You fill a bucket drop by drop. You clear your mind thought by thought. You heal yourself moment by moment. Today I make one drop, clear one thought, and get present to one moment. And then I do it again."
>
> **—Lisa Wimberger**

You can rediscover your unique magic and begin living from it once you create space to become present.

Not one of us is the same, but we live as if we are. It's no surprise that we slowly lose our inherent magic and dim our lights. Many thought leaders and scientists alike have made it loud and clear that through our education system, society, and the media, we can feel forced to live a life devoid of greatness.

Do you remember all the imagination and play when you were young? What if you could tap into that, not just as a memory, but truly feel it? You can.

If you clear your mind from unnecessary noise (should dos, negative self-talk, self-doubt, junk food content, etc.), you are free to reconnect with the spirit within.

Once you make it a priority to reacquaint yourself with your inner self (because you have the time and mental clarity), you can discover what your spirit longs to do, contribute to the greater society, feel, and accomplish.

# Week 1

## The Daily Purge

> "Once we get those muddy, maddening, confusing thoughts [nebulous worries, jitters, and preoccupations] on the page, we face our day with clearer eyes."
>
> **—Julia Cameron**

Given that 80 percent of our thoughts are harmful, and **95 percent** are repetitive, let's wipe the slate clean every morning. In her popular book *The Artist's Way*, Julia Cameron suggests writing three pages of unedited stream of thought every morning. While I think writing is an amazing way of purging, if you rather sing off or dance off or walk off or swim off or run off your negative stream of consciousness, please do so. Just make sure that you do so by yourself and for no less than six minutes a day. More is okay, but I wouldn't do so for more than thirty minutes, as it isn't necessary and then becomes time consuming.

The Daily Purge is an activity you do to release whatever muckety muck is in your mind and clear the slate for your day. Every day you will engage in this very doable activity that will prepare your body, mind, heart, and soul to make massive changes. But the commitment won't be more than a few minutes and can fit into even the busiest of schedules. The specific activity is up to you—writing, doodling, singing, dancing, jogging—but the ONLY intention is to purge. Start every single morning with this six-minute purge: write for six, walk for six, run naked in the woods for six. Before you begin, set the intention to purge every piece of information you've acquired in the last twenty-four hours that tells you who you are supposed to be. Spend six minutes getting rid of it however you'd like...and completely. The Daily Purge is most successful when done every day regardless of what other activities you're doing, and I suggest you continue to do it long after finishing this book. You will come to enjoy it as a daily gift to yourself.

During this time, you cannot strategize, plan your day, work through an issue, create a laundry list, etc. If you find your mind tempted to plan, bring your thought and intention back to the exercise—which is purely to purge and release. Choose whatever activity helps you purge the best. For me it's walking. I always make time to fit in a walk every day. Depending on whether it's a workday or weekend (work days are also usually school days), I'll either walk in the morning or evening. In the mornings on weekends, I'll go near the water on our dock and meditate (after my coffee). My wife, Tracey, makes a fabulous breakfast and then we go for a long walk, often getting into deep philosophical conversations. We do a lot of walking and talking.

My second favorite activity is dancing. I love putting on house music or '80s music and dancing like nobody's watching and often no one is watching (thankfully).

If you're not sure what activity to choose, pick one and try it on for a few days, and if you don't like it, then try a different one. The Daily Purge can help you form healthier habits without making you feel you're just adding another thing to your to-do list.

# Week 1

Exercise: Clearing the Mind Clutter

> "You are the sky. Everything else—it's just the weather."
>
> **—Pema Chödrön**

In addition to the Daily Purge, I've included quick daily exercises. I've done this so that you can experience this book and not just read it. Getting something conceptually and feeling it experientially are vastly different. These exercises won't fix your life in a day or a week. The point of these exercises is to learn to extract your thoughts about what you're learning, move those thoughts onto paper, and apply them to your life. For the first week, you will engage in Brain Detox exercises each day—in addition to the Daily Purge. Each day, I'd like you to journal (or doodle—whatever suits your fancy) using these prompts throughout your first week of brain detox. For each exercise, set your timer for at least six minutes; feel free to go longer, but not beyond thirty minutes.

**Day One:**     What creative activity makes you feel alive and joyful? Schedule time to engage in the activity for at least six minutes. (Suggestions are: writing poetry, telling jokes, drawing a picture, singing songs, dancing, etc.) Then, journal a few more sentences about how this activity made you feel. What were your reactions? (Possible answers: smiling, relaxing, laughing.)

**Day Two:**     What thoughts did you observe this week? Were your reactions to these unbiased? Sit with your thoughts for at least six minutes without judgment. See what comes, what repeats, what lingers. Be aware that you are observing your thoughts. If you're able to observe your thoughts, you have been successful in creating a space between your thoughts and your observation. The more you are able to step into this space, the more you realize you are not your thoughts. When people talk about consciousness or awareness, it is repeatedly stepping into this space.

**Day Three:**   Remember, making time to center yourself is key in decluttering your mind! Spend at least six minutes in complete silence observing the here and now. Thoughts will come and go. Try not to attach to any of them and be present to what is happening in the exact moment. If you're walking, observe what is around you: the trees, the birds, the ground under your feet, the sounds around you, your breath, etc. If you're cooking, observe the way you cut vegetables, the way you add seasoning, how you mix, and so on. Be in the exact moment, and keep bringing yourself back to the here and now for at least six minutes.

**Day Four:** Visualize life exactly as you'd like it to be. You may be rolling your eyes right now, but the truth is that our minds make up stories all the time...and I mean *all* the time. So why not guide it...paint it the way you want. Visualize the person you want to be, the relationships you'd like to have, the community you want to be surrounded with, the people you want to meet, the places you want to travel, the work you want to do, the adventures you want to have, the dreams you want to realize. Do this for at least six minutes. If other thoughts come in—and I guarantee that they will come in—just usher them out, and continue to visualize. If you want it to be longer than six minutes and can afford to do so, then by all means visualize away! The truth is that if you tell your mind something enough times, it will believe it, and if it believes it, you will act accordingly. More on this in Week 6.

**Day Five:** Read your favorite childhood book. If you have it or can get a hard copy fairly easily, it would be preferred, as you would physically hold it in your hands (and remain unplugged). It may sound silly, and maybe even a waste of time, but trust me! There is no faster way to shift your mind than to indulge in the joy of immersing yourself in the world you reveled in as a child. My go-to is *The Adventures of Tintin.* I used to devour the Tintin collection as a child. I read them over and over again whenever I could. As I read, I would instantly become Tintin on all sorts of worldly adventures along with my trusted sidekick pooch, Milou (Snowy in the English version), my friend the Captain, and fellow investigators, Thomson and Thomson. Interestingly enough, a few years ago I took the kids to Belize for vacation, and a few days in, we were stuck in a hurricane. The kids were still quite young and the night the hurricane landed we were in a dense jungle in a gorgeous cottage that resembled something out of the set of Tarzan. The biggest issue was that there were no walls in the main room, just screens. When the hurricane hit, I had the kids climb in bed with me. They were visibly afraid. I was too, but I couldn't let on. I kept having visions of a tree falling on the cottage or something massive flying through the screens. I then made an executive decision to drag the mattress into the bathroom, the only place with walls, and stay there until the hurricane passed. So, from about 1:30 a.m. to around 4:30 a.m. I told the kids one Tintin story after another. I was surprised how easily I could recall and retell the stories. It brought me as much comfort as it brought them, if not more. The hurricane was just another Tintin adventure we were on. Our hurricane adventure didn't end there, but it saved us from one of the most traumatic nights of our lives.

**Day Six:** Be in gratitude. Even if you've had a rough day, crappy week, someone cut you off while driving, you're stressed out about money, or exhausted from work, think of everything you are grateful for. Maybe it's your partner or spouse, your children, your parents, your health, your wealth, your community, the opportunities you've been given, and so on. If you're able to say them out loud, do so. If you can shout or sing them out, even better. If you can't, write them down. Don't worry about spelling or grammar, just write it down. One of my favorite things to do is a gratitude dance. It takes no skill and if anyone could see me, they would probably think I have lost my mind. I just dance around singing, "Thank you, thank you, thank you!" You can do so while sitting, standing, or lying down.

**Day Seven:** Find a guided meditation and follow it— even if you've never meditated before and even if it is just for six minutes (longer if you'd like). This is only an introduction to meditation to prime you for beginning your own practice. We will dive deeper in Week 5, Finding Your True North. There are many, many guided meditations available free or for purchase. Apps abound, as do books and recordings online and in streaming services.*

*Important: I realize I've suggested you unplug this week. This is day seven, and by this time you should have enough mental space and discipline to reintroduce a brief (six to ten minutes) into your routine to ready you for Week 2, Heart Detox. If you wish to still remain unplugged, here is a transcription you can read softly to yourself.

**Resting in Awareness Exercise:** I like to say that the Resting in Awareness Exercise is almost like a meditation hack or a mini meditation, because you can really do it anywhere.

I have often done this exercise at stoplights—the longer ones. I've done it in grocery lines. I do it sometimes when I'm walking alone. What's really beautiful and powerful about it is after you've done it a few times, you can get to that space once you know it much quicker. Meditation is like riding a bike: once you know what that feeling of balance is, you can recognize it easier.

Michael Singer and Eckhart Tolle often tell their followers to step back from your thoughts. That's what you do instantly with resting awareness. You step outside of your thoughts, or behind them, and be. You are aware of this stillness and peace that is, and everything else is buzzing around it. The resting is in that peaceful space, and everyone has it. It's just a matter of stepping behind the thoughts, the garbage, the anxiety, and the panic and all of that.

When situations of conflict arise, I do this exercise. Instead of reacting, I pause. Instead of choosing to engage or debate, I choose to step back. As a parent, I do this all the time. Not so much now, but a few years ago it was a little rough when my son was stepping into adolescence, as we used to butt heads a lot. I had read this meme or a cartoon that said, "They act like sharks, but they're really goldfish." Something would happen and I would say, "They're goldfish.... They're goldfish." There were plenty of times I could have reacted to something he was doing—like talking back to me—and I would pause and sometimes leave the room to recenter rather than engage.

So here is the exercise (given to me by my spiritual coach, Lisa Mansfield):

"I want to encourage you to find a comfortable place to sit and close your eyes and just take a couple of nice deep breaths. And on the out-breath, just begin letting your body relax a little bit more deeply. You want to just take note of how the body feels welcoming, whatever is arising.

Then just noticing what is arising in the emotional realm, allowing everything to be, as it is—allowing all thought forms, all sensations, all the emotions, relaxing your whole system and letting everything be as it is.

And then taking your attention, focus your attention on the awareness that is aware. Noticing that there is awareness that is centered on my voice. There is awareness that is present to your breathing. Let your system relax even more deeply in that restful spacious place of awareness.

That restful place, that spacious space that is wide open, eternal, whole, complete, an emanation of pure love. Let your whole system relax there.

Just taking a moment to remind yourself, 'I am, that I am. My true nature is this awareness in a vast wide-open, undying awareness... this is my true nature.'

And I can just drop into this restful place at any time throughout the day, short

*moments repeated over and over dropping
into that spaciousness and allowing the
display of thought forms and emotions just to
pass through.*

*Everything just comes up in awareness and
then begins dropping away. The stable ground
is your very own awareness. So just return to
that over and over throughout the day."*

Here is a great reference for guided meditations:

You've just finished your first week, which I consider the hardest. It's not just because our monkey minds are very clever at F'ing with us, but because the first steps of any new venture/adventure are often the hardest and scariest. Don't ask me why but I learned how to drive a car with a stick shift. I remember being in an empty parking lot with my mom teaching me how to drive. I had a heck of a time putting the car in first, and I will always remember her saying, "First and reverse are the hardest gears." I've found that to be a great parable for life—the first step is often the most difficult, and going in reverse should only be done when absolutely necessary. Now we can gently shift the gear to the second week: detoxing your heart.

# Week 2

Heart Detox

> "The resting place of the mind is the heart. The only thing the mind hears all day is clanging bells and noise and argument, and all it wants is quietude. The only place the mind will ever find peace is inside the silence of the heart. That's where you need to go."
>
> **—Elizabeth Gilbert**

## SET APART YOUR HEART FROM YOUR HEAD

Now that you've cleared your mind, it's time to detox your heart because, well, your heart really deserves it... and needs it. Once you've read through the chapter, you'll understand why and will hopefully agree with me. At this point, you probably have a good sense of how incredibly resourceful and yet destructive our brains can be. While the mind is quite useful for operations—driving, paying bills, planning, researching, calculating, etc.—it can really mess with your heart. And while thoughts and emotions are very closely tied, they are not the same.

The mind is constantly judging, reviewing, evaluating, calculating, criticizing, spinning. On the other hand, the heart is like a young child or a little puppy wanting nothing more than to be held and accepted for what it is.

We often hear the heart referred to as our "inner child," and it is very much that. I refrain from calling it that because "inner child" sounds too "woo woo" and rather cliche. But your heart truly is your child within. The "younger self" is more accurate. It's not about caring for any child; it's about caring for *oneself* as a child. This alone makes the experience much more intimate and personal. But let's go with "the puppy inside" instead. It's a cute analogy and incredibly accurate.

What the heart desires and needs the most is love and guidance. But not necessarily from another. The heart needs your love first and foremost. What it is, is pure love. That's why they say, "You can't love someone else until you love yourself." And I would argue you can't live a full life unless you love yourself first.

Please know that in this book, there is no right or wrong way to do anything nor a scolding or criticism of how you live or what you have done in the past. So, dive in with your good, your bad, and your ugly. All are accepted here.

Can your heart detox in a week? I believe so, *if* you can promise (to yourself) to take care of it throughout this week and beyond.

# YOUR HEART IS CALLING OUT FOR YOU

> "When you give your heart the room it needs to speak, it will."
>
> **—Cyndie Spiegel**

We all want to feel seen, heard, and loved—unconditionally—as humanly possible. The issue is that we often seek these things outside of ourselves and it becomes a never-ending need that not only puts your heart at the mercy of others, but it puts misplaced responsibility on your loved ones. I am not saying they should not matter. They clearly do and will, but don't look to them to love you big until you love yourself big first.

Until we decide to love ourselves (remember the puppy vying for your attention inside?), we will walk around like a lost little puppy, with a gaping hole. We can't expect our loved ones to fill that void. You are the only one who can soothe the puppy.

## YOUR HEART NEEDS HEALING

> "Someone I loved once gave me a box full of darkness. It took me years to understand that this too, was a gift."
>
> **—Mary Oliver**

Regardless of who you are and what you've gone through, your heart has been broken, disappointed, confused, torn, and lonely. To what degree depends on what you've allowed it to be open to and experience. There is no good or bad, right or wrong here—it just is what it is. This is why a heart detox is important. It's very hard to heal a heart that is heavy with having been broken, disappointed, confused, torn, and lonely.

After my breakup, as uncomfortable as everything (and I really mean every single thing) felt, I knew that if I didn't spend time truly grieving the loss of my partnership and friendship of twenty-two years and my family (as I had known it), that I would be paying the anger, confusion, and sadness forward to my next partner...which is THE most unloving and selfish thing one can do. So, I sat and sat and sat with my grief...and made friends with it. No one was allowed to tell me to get on with it or decide how long I needed to do so.

Healing your heart doesn't mean you put everything and everyone on pause until you've healed it. It means giving it attention, protecting it from people who won't honor it, listening to what it needs, and providing for it, holding it, and letting it know that all will be well. Think of the puppy who just wants to be loved. Love it no matter what you're doing and/or how busy you are. That puppy is lost, lonely, and utterly helpless without you.

## FEEL ALL THE FEELS

There is a whole spectrum of emotions, such as feeling lonely, hurt, frustrated, envious, jealous, regret, and grief. These "complex emotions" are made up of two or more of the basic emotions.

Think of your basic emotions like the RGB colors of your TV.[12] The red, green, and blue when combined in all sorts of hues and patterns make up real life colors. You take one of them away, and the colors are no longer fully representative.

In other words, you need all your emotions in order to completely show up in full technicolor. And understanding which of the emotions or combination of emotions you are feeling will serve you as you work through them...and if you choose, to release them.

A widely accepted theory of basic emotions and their expressions, developed by Paul Ekman, suggests we have six basic emotions. They include sadness, happiness, fear, anger, surprise, and disgust.[13]

---

12  "RGB color model," Wikipedia, edited November 12, 2022, https://en.wikipedia.org/wiki/RGB_color_model.

13  "What are emotions?," Universal Emotions, accessed November 16, 2022, https://www.paulekman.com/universal-emotions/.

I want to take a deeper dive into this theory and explore how these feelings can help you own your power, find your purpose, and live a more balanced, peaceful life. This is the magic you've been anticipating, hidden in the most unlikely of places—like so-called negative feelings such as sadness and anger. Let's dive in.

## Sadness

> "When you are sorrowful, look again in your heart, and you shall see that in truth you are weeping for that which has been your delight."
>
> **—Kahlil Gibran**

Sadness: *n.* an emotional state characterized by feelings of disappointment, grief or hopelessness.

Interestingly enough, the best visual demonstration of the emotional process I can think of, and for sadness in particular, caught me by surprise. At the time Pixar's *Inside Out* came out, my kids were quite young and really wanted to see it. I took them to the theater expecting another heartwarming children's movie. I was not prepared to have my mind blown. It is literally one of the most profound and brilliant films I have ever seen, and I say this having been a snobby film student and a very loyal artsy film festival devotee for many years.

Through the movie, we see the world through the mind of eleven-year-old Riley, as her family relocates from Minnesota to California; in one scene in particular, Riley shares a memory about her home back in the Midwest and how they loved playing ice hockey.

The main character dissolves into a blubbery, sobbing mess. And Joy—the emotional character that thinks everything needs to be just rainbows and butterflies with no ebb and flow of emotions—rushes in to try to help the situation.

It's then we realize that Sadness needs Joy and Joy needs Sadness. The emotions work together for our good, or against us. When I took my then-young kids to see this film, I was struck by how much it moved not just them, but me. It was still the early days of my journey, and I was somewhere in the denial and disbelief stage of my grieving. The film so brilliantly validated so much for me. We are whole beings, and we need a whole plethora of feelings.

Sadness isn't a bad thing. It shouldn't be avoided. It should be embraced. In small doses, unless the circumstance demands that you grieve hard. Like the death of a relationship. Been there, done that.

> "There is nothing quite so satisfying,
> and so healing, as a good cry."
>
> **—Leo Buscaglia**

Sadness Purge (optional): If you're feeling sad, instead of repressing it or ignoring it, invite it in for as long as you can. Invite it in, play music for it, sway with it, cuddle it, and when you feel ready, tell it that it is okay to go...and then release it. It may come back (a few more times) and when it does, do the same thing. What you resist persists.

## Happiness

> "Is there a difference between happiness and inner peace?.... Happiness depends on conditions being perceived as positive; inner peace does not."
>
> **—Eckhart Tolle**

**Happiness:** *n.* the quality or state of being happy. Good fortune; pleasure; contentment; joy.

To answer Eckhart Tolle's question in my own words: yes, happiness is fleeting. Inner peace is not.

Arguably, happiness is not exactly an emotion; it is a pleasant emotional state that elicits feelings of joy, contentment, and satisfaction. It could rather be more akin to contentment, which is more like a relationship with your life. Happiness, like Joy in that movie *Inside Out*, is tightly connected to each one of the other emotions. Joy (the emotion, not the character) is further on the "happy spectrum," though, than happiness. That's because, as they say, happiness is fleeting. I tend to agree with this.

The work you're doing here on yourself will naturally lead to more happy moments throughout your life, despite the circumstances you endure. Because peace, lasting contentment, and joy do not need to be circumstantial. They can be generated and sustained by working out your heart muscle.

Honestly, though, I have found more sustainable contentment when I came to the realization that I don't have to be jubilant 24/7. Other emotions, as we've discussed, are equally important to feel the rhythm of life. We can't sing the same song all the time, and we can't be happy all the time either! That would be unnatural. There is an ebb and flow to emotions.

Society gives us pressure to "be happy," and it's impossible to do that. It's a misnomer. Peace and contentment are what can be achieved, though, closer to most of the time. The quest for eternal "happiness" is bound to bring disappointments. In life, there are no fairy tales where everyone lives happily ever after. And that is a good thing! That would be boring.

In life, we need ups and downs so that we can grow. We need cruxes and make-or-break moments because those seemingly scary moments can lead to the best breakthroughs. We need complex emotions. We don't need to complicate life further by striving daily to put on a fake smile and pretend that we're happy when we're not.

Inner peace should be your goal on this journey.

## Fear

Fear: *n.* a basic, intense emotion aroused by the detection of imminent threat, involving an immediate alarm reaction that mobilizes the organism by triggering a set of physiological changes. These include rapid heart-beat, redirection of blood flow away from the periphery toward the gut, tensing of the muscles, and a general mobilization of the organism to take action (fight or flight)[14]

Fear and worry go hand and hand. And often, they team up together to steal your peace and put in its place worry. The purpose of the feeling of fear is to make us act. To run, to be anxious. Think fight-or-flight response.[15] This response was necessary in evolution, but not necessary in most cases now. And when this becomes too built up in our system, that's when fear becomes worry and takes over.

Combatting fear is a conscious choice to choose love, instead of fear. Fear runs much deeper than just a biological response that we have to manage or attempt to block. **Fear is the exact opposite of love.** If fear is present, love cannot exist. We hold too tightly on to the fear to allow love to flow. The heart inside can't beat freely if fear has a stranglehold. So, we have to loosen that stronghold, for ourselves and others. We gotta let that puppy run free, not be bound by the chains of fear.

Failing to do so leads to very harmful byproducts. Fear breeds hate and misunderstanding. That hate then breeds more fear. It's this horrible, toxic, cyclical nature of fear that can lead to homophobia, racism, etc.

Fear and its byproducts are highly destructive powers that we have to deactivate within us before it spreads like

---

14   American Psychological Association, "APA Dictionary of Psychology," https://dictionary.apa.org/fear.

15   Kendra Cherry, "What Is the Fight-or-flight Response?," verywellmind, updated November 7, 2022, https://www.verywellmind.com/what-is-the-fight-or-flight-response-2795194.

the transmission of an infectious disease, spoiling our inner selves and exponentially—eventually—society at large.

"Our deepest fear is not that we are inadequate. Our deepest fear is that we are powerful beyond measure. It is our light, not our darkness that most frightens us. We ask ourselves, 'Who am I to be brilliant, gorgeous, talented, fabulous?' Actually, who are you not to be? You are a child of God. Your playing small does not serve the world. There is nothing enlightened about shrinking so that other people won't feel insecure around you. We are all meant to shine, as children do. We were born to make manifest the glory of God that is within us. It's not just in some of us; it's in everyone. And as we let our own light shine, we unconsciously give other people permission to do the same. As we are liberated from our own fear, our presence automatically liberates others."

**—Marianne Williamson, *A Return to Love: Reflections on the Principles of "A Course in Miracles"***

Fear, regret, and anxiety also go hand in hand. These emotions are all made up unless the stimuli is happening in the present. Meaning, if there is a regret of something, it is a memory. If it is a memory, it's not right now. If it is anxiety about something in the past or the future, we're missing out on the possibility to be mindful and thus positive now. Our minds are powerful, and our imagination—though equally as manipulative—is just purely made up. If it has not, is not, or will not happen, it's not worth our energy. In most cases, it's stealing our energy when we could otherwise be using it for good.

Fear Purge (optional): Years ago, I used to have this recurring dream/nightmare that some alien force would levitate my body from my bed to the ceiling. Every time I would be lifted, I would go into a major panic, and I'd keep my eyes closed as I was getting closer and closer until I would wake up drenched in sweat. When I shared this story with my ex, she suggested that I open my eyes when I reach the ceiling. As frightening as that sounded, I did so and woke up instantly...never to have that nightmare again. I think it serves as a great metaphor. When fear arises, see if you can meet it with as much love as possible, look at it as courageously as you can, and ask it what it needs and why it is there. It may be there to teach you something or in facing it, you may realize you no longer have it. If fear is truly the opposite of love, then fill that space with as much love as possible over and over and over again.

# Anger

> "Anger is like flowing water; there's nothing wrong with it as long as you let it flow. Hate is like stagnant water; anger that you denied yourself the freedom to feel, the freedom to flow; water that you

> gathered in one place and left to forget. Stagnant water becomes dirty, stinky, disease-ridden, poisonous, deadly; that is your hate. On flowing water travels little paper boats; paper boats of forgiveness. Allow yourself to feel anger, allow your waters to flow, along with all the paper boats of forgiveness. Be human."
>
> **—C. JoyBell C.**

**Anger:** *n.* an emotion characterized by tension and hostility arising from frustration, real or imagined injury by another, or perceived injustice.[16]

We all get mad at times. But being mad for a moment and being in a perpetual cynical cycle is when anger takes over. It's okay to feel feelings. I meant it when I said feel all the feelings. Anger is no exception. Anger can easily take over and make us bitter if we don't catch ourselves in that cycle of cynicism though. We can become a critic of everything.

Have you ever been so tired that you couldn't see straight? And you were cranky like a toddler, and everything made you agitated? A typical toddler will at some point learn to throw their sippy cup down to have their caretaker pick it up for giggles. That same toddler may discover—on a day that they missed their much-needed nap—that even when you provide them with the perfectly

---

16    American Psychological Association, "APA Dictionary of Psychology," https://dictionary.apa.org/anger.

made favorite lunch of PB&J or whatever, they will throw a fit because nothing will pacify them except for a nap. This is an example of anger driving the wheel.

If you want to have more peace and more positive feelings, and find your purpose and fully step into it, limiting angry feelings is a necessary step.

To just usher out your anger is not enough. We have to channel it. We have to let anger fuel our fire, not for hate, but to create positive change. How can this be accomplished? It already has been, in droves. Look at the Me Too and Black Lives Matter movements of the second decade of the twenty-first century. These movements were rooted in deep, systemic hate that came from generations of otherwise loving souls misunderstanding others and eventually becoming bound and controlled by fear.

Changing the status quo, when it no longer serves the masses nor the minority, comes about when people—one by one—decide to choose love over anger. The silence, the inequality, and injustice are brought to the surface by loving souls who won't stand by any longer. Anger is catalyzed to create much needed and welcomed widespread change.

> "Anybody can become angry—that is easy; but to be angry with the right person, and to the right degree, and at the right time, and for the right purpose, and in the right way—that is not within everybody's power and is not easy."
>
> **—Aristotle**

"Anger is just anger. It isn't good. It isn't bad. It just is. What you do with it is what matters. It's like anything else. You can use it to build or to destroy. You just have to make the choice."

**—Jim Butcher, *White Night***

## Surprise

**Surprise:** *n.* an emotion typically resulting from the violation of an expectation or the detection of novelty in the environment[17]

Intense feelings—like surprise—have the power to activate our energy. Intensifying and invigorating feelings like surprise feel like a jolt to the system. An email from a supervisor asking for a report that was due that you weren't aware of or dropped the ball on. A late-night plea from your child to help with her due (or worse, overdue) science experiment. A last-minute invite to an exciting event you thought you were going to miss out on. In these moments, our physiology actually changes. Time stands still. Our bodies can physically freeze (as we jump or hold our breath).[18]

---

17    American Psychological Association, "APA Dictionary of Psychology," https://dictionary.apa.org/surprise.

18    Kristen Meinzer and T.J. Raphael, "Here's what happens after 'Surprise!'," Podcast, *The World*, April 2, 2015, https://www.pri.org/stories/2015-04-02/heres-what-happens-after-surprise#:~:text=Surprises%20actually%20cause%20humans%20to,figure%20out%20what%20is%20happening

We can use this energy to our advantage too! The hormone adrenaline is released in our bodies also, just as it does with anger, when we're surprised. It's that flutter in your stomach, that immediate breaking out in sweats, and that missed breath. Adrenaline and other similar hormones have also been documented to increase cognitive ability.[19]

How does this work? Well, I have been super interested in neuroplasticity since I started my spiritual journey. Here's a quick breakdown. Neuroplasticity basically means how our neural pathways reorganize in our minds. Over time, as we commit to learning new things, and memorize those new things, we experience physiological changes within our minds and increase our ability to retain and recall information.[20] We will be diving deeper into neuroscience and neuroplasticity in Week 4.

The hormone norepinephrine—very similar to adrenaline—can increase in the body and leads to heightened mental focus, memory retention, and memory recall in the mind. It's worth underscoring once again: seemingly so-called intense or negative emotions can be used to increase our power and thus our magical powers!

---

19    Jerry Bower, "Looking For A Cognitive Enhancer? Skip The Drugs And Try Fasting Instead," *Forbes*, January 6, 2017, https://www.forbes.com/sites/jerrybowyer/2017/01/06/looking-for-a-cognitive-enhancer-skip-the-drugs-and-try-fasting-instead/?sh=7f0d49374592

20    Jay W. Marks, MD, "Medical Definition of Neuroplasticity," MedicineNet, reviewed June 3, 2021, https://www.medicinenet.com/neuroplasticity/definition.htm

# Disgust

> **Disgust:** *n.* a strong aversion, for example, to the taste, smell, or touch of something deemed revolting, or toward a person or behavior deemed morally repugnant[21]

The physical discomfort and nausea that come with this feeling are palpable. This can come in one of two ways. This feeling can arise when we are subjected to things that don't align with our beliefs or when we are made to endure things that make us extremely physically uncomfortable.[22]

Many times, this is a gut reaction. Think of "getting the willies" or "having the heebie jeebies." It's that state of nervousness or anxiety that makes us sweat, shake, or want to be sick. This can be an extreme reaction, like when you watch a horror flick or see someone who truly broke your heart. It could also occur when you witness injustice or, worse, are the victim of it.

Powerful emotions, like we've discussed with anger, have the potential to motivate us to change—on the personal and interpersonal level. Engaging with disgust is much like taking stock of thoughts as they come into your mind. You can become curious about why you are feeling this way, if it's not clear.

---

21 American Psychological Association, "APA Dictionary of Psychology," https://dictionary.apa.org/disgust.

22 "Disgust," Universal Emotions, accessed November 16, 2022, https://www.paulekman.com/universal-emotions/what-is-disgust/#:~:-text=Disgust%20is%20one%20of%20the,people%2C%20and%20even%20by%20ideas.

These unpleasant feelings serve a meaningful purpose, if we allow them. It is our response that determines whether or not we step into that. Even a memory that doesn't ever seem to leave you will weigh you down with disgust. So, confronting the feeling, exploring the reasoning behind it, and allowing—*not accepting*—the feelings is how you feel this feeling without letting it hurt you beyond repair.

## LET THE FEELINGS PASS THROUGH YOU, DON'T LET THEM CONTROL YOU

You're going to feel how you feel when you feel the feels regardless of how much "transformational" work you do. The same way you can't control the thoughts that come into your mind but you can choose which ones you feed, emotions will come and go as they please. But we have a tremendous (and yet seldom used) ability to transform negative feelings into mental and emotional power. Let's use anger as an example, since it's one of the most strongly felt emotions and the easiest to recognize. We all get angry, but how many times, while angry, have you thought to yourself, *How do I process this?* The first step, you guessed it: invite it in, pour it some tea, and sit with it—without reacting.

It can be tough to do this because adrenaline, a hormone released during the fight-or-flight response, is a very powerful influence on our minds, hearts, bodies, souls—the whole gamut. It's been documented to give humans superpowers to move cars in order to save babies and other monumental things like severing off a limb while crushed. It also has the power to immobilize you, even in the midst of only perceived threat.

But if you commit to just feeling the anger and not letting it *control* you—thereby, processing it—you can begin using it as a catalyst for a more powerful purpose. Your anger and your fear are fuel for your power. Moving past anger will give you empathy, help you see the world with more enlightened eyes, and give you peace at times when it's unexplainable. That power, that anger, which was meant to harm you (and your relationships) can now be used to increase your mental and emotional power. Now that's really loving yourself big.

Because of the work you've been doing in this book (hopefully), you have a renewed mind, and there is room to listen to yourself about the anger you've felt. You can redirect that powerful energy back toward yourself, but flipping it around so it's invigorating, not draining. Since you've rearranged your previously misaligned beliefs, anytime anger tries to have an extended stay in your heart again, you can use the power of your mind to redirect it out of your being.

It's how we dance with all the emotions and what we do with them that makes all the difference, but it is important to not reject any. Bottling up emotions is never a good idea! It's that boiling up that has the potential to overtake you without you even realizing. Suppressing emotions—good and bad—is detrimental to your overall health on all levels, because we are beings who are meant to be.

We are meant to explore emotion, to exude it, to share it. Over time, not emitting emotions, or even not admitting them, can cause the physical manifestation of stress. Feelings can manifest physically, emotionally, mentally, and spiritually. We can put a block on positive vibes by not letting emotions flow. A study by the University of Texas found that by not acknowledging feelings, we actually make them stronger within us![23]

An alternative I've found that truly works to strengthen and steady me is to harness that power. It grounds me to my purpose and gives me guardrails for how I interact with my inner feelings. We can't entertain the puppy's every whim and expect it to ever be a good companion, can we? The heart is the same.

---

23  "Can Always Staying Positive Be Bad for Our Health?" Health Agenda, accessed December 2022, https://www.hcf.com.au/health-agenda/body-mind/mental-health/downsides-to-always-being-positive#:~:text=%E2%80%9CSuppressing%20your%20emotions%2C%20whether%20it's,physical%20stress%20on%20your%20body.&text=And%20avoiding%20emotions%20can%20also,aggression%2C%20anxiety%20and%20depression%E2%80%9D.

# The Guest House[24]

This being human is a guest house.
Every morning a new arrival.
A joy, a depression, a meanness,
some momentary awareness comes
As an unexpected visitor.
Welcome and entertain them all!
Even if they're a crowd of sorrows,
who violently sweep your house
empty of its furniture,
still treat each guest honorably.
He may be clearing you out
for some new delight.
The dark thought, the shame, the malice,
meet them at the door laughing,
and invite them in.
Be grateful for whoever comes,
because each has been sent
as a guide from beyond.

**—Rumi**

This exercise in feeling feelings doesn't equate to entertaining them. It also doesn't mean you have to act every time you feel something, but it is important to let them in, recognize them, and determine what you want to do with the feelings, just as you decide what to do with your

---

24    Rumi, translated by Coleman Barks, "The Guest House," https://all-poetry.com/poem/8534703-The-Guest-House-by-Mewlana-Jalaluddin-Rumi

thoughts. The mind and the heart work together—against, or for you. You decide.

Psychologists agree that what we resist persists,[25] so I argue we should deny nothing and acknowledge everything. That, of course, does not equate to entertaining or acting on every thought. Remember what we covered about the mind and thoughts: we have a thought, we do not have to have it have us!

## DON'T LET YOUR HEART LEAD YOU

I'm sure you've heard the phrase "Let your heart lead" or other variations like "Follow your heart." Don't listen to this advice! That is misguided advice that's sadly been widely accepted. What the saying should be is "Let your soul lead." Not the heart.

Why? Because the heart is a very fickle thing. The heart is a child, or our example here, a puppy. And the heart always will be. It is what keeps you pure with integrity. It is kind, loving, playful, vulnerable...and finicky. Would you let a puppy run rampant in your life?

The guidance of the complex tapestry of our life can't be left to the heart. The intricately interwoven decisions and actions should be guided by a complex team of your mind, heart, body, soul, and Higher Power. Not a puppy.

The best illustration I can think of beyond the puppy is driving my kids to school. At the writing of this book, my two children attend schools in my ex's school district. From her house, it takes ten minutes to get to my son's

25    Jessica Schrader, "You Only Get More of What You Resist—Why?" *Psychology Today*, June 15, 2016, https://www.psychologytoday.com/us/blog/evolution-the-self/201606/you-only-get-more-what-you-resist-why.

high school and twenty minutes to get to my daughter's middle school. From my house, it takes thirty minutes and forty minutes, respectively. They're great schools, worth the commitment. In order for them to be on time for their first class, we have to wake up at 5:50 a.m. so we can be out the door by 6:50 a.m.

So many mornings when I have to wake up at 5:50 a.m., I simply don't want to. I would honestly much rather get more sleep and stay in my cozy bed at home. But I love my kids. And I want better for them. So, I don't let either my heart or body lead in that instance. It's my higher commitment to my children—which has "soul" written all over it—that gets me out of bed every time.

If you left it up to your heart (that very cute, big-eyed puppy), one day it would feel like doing something, the next day not so much. Then the next day after that, it will feel sad and won't wanna. Still, the next it will—because it's happy again. Until the next day, it's angry. You get my point. Don't let your mind, heart, or body lead. The ONLY exception to this is if your mind, heart, or body need rest. Then, by all means, let them lead and rest. Your soul will let you know regardless, but we're just at the stage of clearing the way to it. More on letting your soul lead in Week 5.

## YOUR HEART NEEDS A TRIBE—NOT EVERYONE IS YOUR PEOPLE

"Our stories are not meant for everyone. Hearing them is a privilege, and we should always ask ourselves this before we share: 'Who has earned the right to hear my story?' If we have one or two people in our lives who can sit with us and hold space for our shame stories, and love us for our strengths and struggles, we are incredibly lucky. If we have a friend, or small group of friends, or family who embraces our imperfections, vulnerabilities, and power, and fills us with a sense of belonging, we are incredibly lucky."

**—Brené Brown**

As homosapiens, we are hardwired to be social. In other words, we are people who need people. The stronger our community, the better our lives. Who you invite in and who you don't is of extreme importance. I've come up with a unique process for handling any relationship in life. But before we dive into that, let's step back and reevaluate the people who have earned the right to be in our tribe. We've all heard the quote "You are the company you keep," but a more accurate quote would be "We are the WAY we interact/keep company with the people in our lives." Yes, we are always in choice, but the choosing is not always so black and white. For example, I do not have a choice in co-parenting with my ex. She *has* to be in my life. She is technically a "company I keep," but she is nowhere close to my heart. So where does she fit? More on this in the next section. For now, let's identify your tribe.

Have you heard of blue zones around the world, where people live the longest and are the healthiest? There are five, to be exact: Okinawa, Japan; Sardinia, Italy; Nicoya, Costa Rica; Ikaria, Greece; and Loma Linda, California. In psychology the color blue symbolizes an introspective journey and represents wisdom and a deeper understanding of the world.[26]

These communities live longer because they grow together, do life together, and essentially create a tribe—a bubble—from the outer world that creates more understanding, more peace, and more productivity—and a lengthier life![27]

The most incredible thing about these communities is that they are home to the largest populations of Centenarians—humans who have lived over a century. Belonging to a community is clearly a key ingredient in the longevity secret sauce.

You can emulate a blue zone without actually moving to one, rather by assembling a tribe.

26    Kate Smith, "Color Symbolism & Meaning of Blue," Sensational Color, accessed November 16, 2022, https://www.sensationalcolor.com/meaning-of-blue/.

27    "5 'Blue Zones' Where the World's Healthiest People Live," *National Geographic*, April 6, 2017, https://www.nationalgeographic.com/books/features/5-blue-zones-where-the-worlds-healthiest-people-live/.

This journey—not just the process in this book, but this journey called life—is not meant to be experienced alone. Yes, there is a great deal of inner work and inner journey, but you need your tribe to support you.

Who is or will be your tribe? These are friends and family members who you trust implicitly. They are the ones who love you big, give of themselves freely, who will love you no matter what, who will listen, and who will make time for you.

If you only have one such person in your life, that is enough, but I've realized that my tribe members fulfill different needs in me.

One person I run so very deep with, that when we connect, we always skip the "Hi" and "How are you" and go directly to the point whenever we speak. Another member of my tribe feeds my heart by allowing us to play together—more on this in Week 4. Another tribe mate is a fellow country mate, so we share a great deal of culture and history together. She is also very heady and feeds my intellect. My sister is another, though sometimes critical (as older sisters can be) she has always and will always have my back...and I hers. I know this instinctively. And my lovely wife, who does a combination of all the above.

The influences we allow ourselves to be affected by sculpt our social reality. Choose your tribe mindfully.

# TASER, SHIELD, FILTER, OR HUG

> "The quality of your life ultimately depends on the quality of your relationships."
>
> **—Esther Perel**

Who expands your heart? Who contracts it? Who do you invite to your table? It's worth going through all the people in your life and figuring out where they belong. I call this "Taser, Shield, Filter, or Hug."

**Taser:** This category is for people who need to stay far away. If they don't need to be in your life, don't let them—not even remotely. This is a group of people that are another "T-word," and no I'm not talking about "too much to handle." I'm talking about people who are toxic to you and your well-being. I want you to take out that imaginary taser and zap them out of your life.

My old boss, for instance, has a huge reputation for being a complete ass. I knew this going into working for him, but at first he showed me a very different side, and I assumed that we would have a very different relationship. Fairly early on, it became clear that he wasn't going to let me do the rebranding and restructuring of the agency that I had been hired to do. Every time I made a move, he moved to block me.

There are only two people I will never *ever* work for again even if you paid me $5 billion, and he would be one of them. *Taser, taser, taser.* I left and cut all ties. But when I walked out, it became the catalyst for creating my own agency. I have him to thank for that.

People like my former boss or someone who abused you, are people who you should choose to not have in your life. If for some reason you have to have these individuals in your life, keep them far, far away. Ignore or block their calls. Simply walk away if they try to engage. This is distinctly different from the next category, Shield.

**Shield:** This category is for people who are in your life, but not welcome to your table...or your personal life. This could be an ex with whom you have to co-parent. My ex currently sits somewhere between Shield and the next category "Filter." For many years, she was squarely seated in the Shield category. If I could have tasered her out of my life, I would have but we were and are bound together in parenting and that had to take precedence. We are much more aligned these days so, depending on the topic and situation, I either shield her from me or filter what I share. Your shield may be for an aunt who you love but is a complete nuisance, a manager whom you have to tolerate, and the like. Set strong boundaries and keep them!

**Filter:** This category is for people you want in your life, but who are not necessarily invited to your inner table. Spending time with these types of people will take a delicate type of control. It's about discerning what you share with people—just because you think it, doesn't mean you have to share it. Honesty is sharing your truth, but this doesn't equate to revealing every passing thought or emotion. Not every single person in your life needs to know everything that you're doing or thinking. Not everything in your life has to be uploaded to Facebook, Instagram, TikTok, LinkedIn, or Snapchat.

**Hug:** This category is for those at your table, those who inspire you: a mentor, a wise friend, an elder, a spiritual leader, etc. The trick here is that you continue to challenge yourself to share with them as openly, vulnerably, and honestly as possible—even when it doesn't make you look good. Bring your confusion, your grief, your disappointment, your goofiness, your seeking here. This is where you are safe to be all shades of you. This is where you step into your true self, to make the most of your time here on Earth with deep, meaningful relationships. This is a way that you love your heart big, and give your heart a hug, as you let cherished loved ones love you and vice versa.

## GIFT YOUR HEART—GET SQUISHY WITH IT

In Week 4 we will spend time exploring the concept of play, which your heart—your younger self or puppy—is starving for. But for now, I ask you to treat your heart with kindness, love, and attention, whenever you can. Making this a priority is an absolute game-changer. It's like making it a priority to walk a puppy each day to help level out their high-energy; same thing applies here. Giving your heart more attention gives your life more balance. You need to play.

In *The Artist's Way*, Julia Cameron asks you to take your inner artist for a date to help you unblock your creativity.[28] In the same vein, I ask you to open up time and space to gift your heart exactly the way you want it to

---

28    Penelope Green, "Julia Cameron Wants You to Do Your Morning Pages," *The New York Times*, February 2, 2019, https://www.nytimes.com/2019/02/02/style/julia-cameron-the-artists-way.html.

be treated, at least once a week. I used to joke that if I were queen of the universe, I would create a magical space where time would open up, say between a Tuesday at 11:59 p.m. and Wednesday at 12:00 a.m. (call it Tuwednesday), and that one minute could last as long as you'd want and you could do whatever you wanted before coming back to your day-to-day life. See if you can give yourself that Tuwednesday, that magical minute. I truly don't know one person in my life who is not time-starved. Even my kids are time-starved! I'm asking you to make the time— that can last a few minutes to a few hours—and really take care of yourself. This could be as simple as reading a new poem, listening to a song that you love, going to a special place, watching your favorite romcom, going to a museum, playing on a swing, splashing in a puddle, dancing your butt off. Whatever that treat may be, do so for your heart's sake. Make your inner puppy giddy... even if for a few minutes.

## GIFT YOUR HEART TO THE WORLD

As you can most likely tell, I am a huge proponent of protecting your heart the same way one would protect a child or puppy. But even through my grief and struggles, there were times where I felt I was overflowing with love and not sure where to put it all. I of course loved my kids, family, friends, neighbors, community, etc...but I still had love to give. Then I discovered Metta—a type of Buddhist meditation where one offers loving kindness to all. Think of it as love volunteering or love altruism. Through Metta, you are offering loving kindness to a world so in need of healing—and regardless of whether you believe a person deserves it or not. It has been one of the most powerful means of expanding and healing my heart. If right now you feel you have no or little heart to give, please don't force yourself to practice Metta. Doing so would defeat the purpose. But if you feel your heart may benefit, please try it. It can be in the form of a sitting meditation or just repeated as you're walking, jogging, cycling, rowing, driving, or whatever. The important thing is to focus on the words spoken, whether out loud or internal. Start with "May I be happy. May I be well. May I be safe. May I be peaceful." Repeat this a few times, and then begin to extend it to someone you care for deeply. Imagine them in your mind and say, "May you be happy. May you be well. May you be safe. May you be peaceful." Repeat this again and see if your feelings become stronger. Now imagine other friends, family, neighbors, strangers, animals, and even people you may not like or agree with. It may be tough to offer to some who have really harmed you, but if you can allow yourself to send them loving kindness regardless, it can be incredibly powerful and healing. This does not mean you are excusing them of any wrongdoing or letting them back into your life. Quite the opposite—you are sending them loving kindness, so the upset, bitterness, and pain are released from you.

As counterintuitive as it may sound and feel, sending Metta to my ex and others I have held in my Shield category has been very healing and powerful. If you can do so with people in your Taser category, then you're one step ahead. You're certainly not obligated to, though.

# Week 2

## The Daily Purge

> "Write it on your heart that every day is
> the best day in the year."
>
> **—Ralph Waldo Emerson**

Each day this week, you will devote your body, mind, heart, and soul to continuing your progress. This (re)vision of your life is an iterative process where you must put in a bit of work to yield incredible results. The minimum time is six minutes, maximum thirty. Engage with this as you see fit. This is all about intentionality and engagement. I hope after week one you have enjoyed this as a daily affirmation that helps you make the most of each moment, hour, and day.

As a reminder, this is your time to purge anything that is weighing you down or brings you pain and angst. Spit it out, shake it out, dance it off, wiggle it out of you.

The most ideal time is the morning. Start every single morning with this six-minute purge: write for six, walk for six, run naked in the woods for six. Before you begin, set the intention to purge every piece of information you've acquired in the last twenty-four hours that tells you who you are supposed to be. Spend six minutes getting rid of it however you'd like...and completely. The Daily Purge is most successful when done every day regardless of what other activities you're doing, and I suggest you continue to do it long after finishing this book. You will come to enjoy it as a daily gift to yourself. During this time, you cannot strategize, plan your day, work through an issue, create a laundry list, etc. If you find your mind tempted to plan, bring your thought and intention back to the exercise— which is purely to purge and release. Choose whatever activity helps you purge the best.

# Week 2

## Exercise: Giving the Lovable Puppy Affection

> "The most sophisticated people I know—
> inside they are all children."
>
> **—Jim Henson**

This week is not just about fixing a broken heart. It's about picking up the pieces and reassembling them to create a heart that beats with purpose. This is about getting your heart *right*, not fighting with your heart. These exercises are designed to find you where you are right now, and help you rescue your own heart from whatever has momentarily broken it. Your heart isn't broken, it's just letting a bit more light in. And with these exercises, you can shine even brighter.

Journal each day (or produce pages of doodles—whatever resonates with your creative sensibilities) using these prompts throughout your second week, Heart Detox.

**Day One:**   Begin to give yourself the love you have desperately needed and deserved but may not have ever received. I want to ask you to bravely confront what may be a triggering memory (a memory that can evoke strong emotion).[29] Here is a quick creative prompt to inspire your work:

- Close your eyes, and think of a time in your childhood when you felt really sad or lonely. Maybe you were scolded or left alone when you didn't want to be. Maybe you wanted attention or affection and did not get it. Now imagine that you are observing yourself as a child.

- You see her or him (who was you) on your childhood bed or in the corner of your childhood bedroom or in the street or at school—wherever you were hurt. Pick the first place that comes to mind, as it is usually the most vivid/important. Observe the younger you in pain. What does she/he need right now? What are the words she/he needs to hear?

- Now walk into that bedroom, house, school, street, or specific location as you are right now and kneel in front of the younger you. She/he is not afraid because she/he recognizes you. Meet her/his eyes, and stay there, looking into your younger eyes.

---

29   "Coping with Memories, Triggers and Reminders," Sutter Health, accessed November 16, 2022, https://www.sutterhealth.org/health/teens/emotions-mental-health/coping-with-memories-triggers-reminders#:~:text=A%20trigger%20is%20a%20feeling,can%20cause%20intense%20physical%20reactions.

- Let her/him know through your gaze that she/he is safe, seen and loved. Then slowly wrap your arms around the younger you, letting her/him rest her/his head on your shoulder, and hold them for a while.

- When you are ready, let the child know that you see her/him, and that you see and feel the hurt, that you are there to keep her/him safe, that you will never leave them alone again...and that all will be well. All will be well.

- As you are holding your younger self, slowly open your eyes, promising never to lose sight of her/him.

**Day Two:**    Begin to heal your heart. Here's a meditation. This one is quite short because others can be more intense. This can be done anywhere, at any time throughout the week, and can be continued as an affirmation. I encourage every reader to read and embrace:

## Short Meditation for Mending the Heart

- Your heart may still be holding on to hurts.

- The younger self will help you recall what you need from this life.

- You can rediscover what you love to do, that you love yourself, and that you can radiate joy.

- Your heart is waiting for you to give it unconditional attention and love.

- Greet your heart with grace and mercy and love.

- Invite peace into your heart.

- Don't see your heart and inner, younger self as broken, see it radiating with light.

- You will begin to feel more bright, less broken, starting today.

**Day Three:** This will be a longer meditation and is really an extension of the first exercise we started. It is taking it one step further so that you focus more on healing, less on triggering emotions. You will be feeling those, if they come, and then releasing those.

- Meditation—Grieving the Past; Greeting the Future

- Allow your body to begin to settle. Find a comfy seat in a chair, on a couch, on a bed, the floor, a porch swing. Whatever feels right.

- Once firmly grounded to the earth, start to feel a sense of calm greet you all over your body.

- Begin releasing any tension you've been holding on to.

- Let your mind drop down into the present moment fully.

- Focus back on your breath.

- Feel your tummy rise and fall.

- Notice the ups and downs of deep breaths.

- Keep your mind focused on your breathing.

- Bring your third, mind eye onto your childhood home or where you had a hurt you've maybe been holding on to.

- If you can picture it, see the details of the outside.

- See the neighborhood if you can.

- Envision yourself on the doorstep, as an adult.

- Now envision you as you are now as an adult, and walk up to the house and hold the hand of your younger self.

- Begin to explore feelings as you explore the home or place.

- Keep focusing on your breathing, and begin to move around the place. Move through the feelings in your mind.

- Allow your breath that's leading you to lift your spirits and settle any sorrow you may have.

- Inhaling as deeply as you can, stay focused on where your mind is taking you.

- Greet anyone in the memory as you greet your younger self.

- Take note of emotions you feel and any vibrations they are emitting.

- Keep a hold of your child's hand gently.

- Walk through the home, then back outside.

- Spin softly around, kneel down to the child version of you, and hug them as you would a relative you hadn't seen in what seems like forever.

- Tell them you love them, you see them, you accept them, that they are favored. And tell them they're safe.

- Tell them that in their new reality, they won't have to be scared anymore. They can be at peace.

- Now walk out of your childhood home, walk into your life.

- Bring your mind back to where you are now.

- Greet your (re)vision of your life.

**Day Four:** In Western culture, we tend to think of letting go or grieving as being linear. The 5 Stages of Grief [30] used to, at one time, be thought of as a process that began and ended. Now, decades later, psychologists realize it is a process that can repeat, especially if the emotional states are not worked through. We can't move on because the reality is that some things never leave us. We have to come to peace with those emotions.

---

30   Jody Clark, MA, LPC/MHSP, "The Five Stages of Grief," verywell-mind, updated July 26, 2022, https://www.verywellmind.com/five-stages-of-grief-4175361.

By choosing to acknowledge the pain and hurts from the past, when new hurts arise, it will lessen the blow. I've found that the pain can more quickly fade away because you've already worked through the grieving process and realize that those emotions don't have to linger forever.

This does not invalidate the fact that you are still feeling sadness/despair/pain, but it does mean that whatever happened before doesn't have to dictate how you feel now. You can stop holding on to what hurt you before, and redirect it by releasing it.

Begin letting go of the past by doing this additional quick exercise:

- Once more, greet the past and release it. You won't say goodbye because letting go is not just a one-time event. It's a choice and a repeated action.

- When the memories or past sweep back into our lives again, you no longer have to feel defeated or deflated. You can feel equipped to greet the feelings and remind your younger self that you are loved and safe and that it's just a memory. And it only has to trigger you if you let it.

- Many times, we are suppressing old feelings and thoughts and ideas from memories that we need to surrender, to feel better. Take some time to sit with your feelings. Conjure up your saddest memory that you haven't already addressed and greet it, then with grace release it.

- Write a farewell letter, poem, song, dance, or even go run, breathing through the release. Begin to feel the weight of all of those feelings that have brought you disgust.

**Day Five:** Sometimes despair holds us up for ransom. Especially sadness coming from fear. And that can lead to confusion becoming our companion. But choosing love will release those feelings. Play your favorite love song and imagine it is being played live, just for you. And feel love so near you can almost feel it hug you.

You can be your biggest helper in your healing process. But you can't keep carrying so-called negative feelings on your shoulders; you have to surrender to rest and rescue yourself from those pains.

> "Life begins on the other side of despair."
>
> **—Jean-Paul Sartre**

Decide today to dance with your sadness. Imagine in your mind that you are in a lovely venue—a dance hall or intimate lounge—whichever you prefer. See your sadness dancing with you. You ask your sadness or similar feeling to dance with you. Sway with it, don't let it lead you. You are the lead. Take the sadness by the hand and hold it tightly, swaying with the music, but when the song is over, let it go.

Here is a song that many find emotional but healing as well:

Day Six:     Refusing to forgive can build a fortress around your heart. To break down those walls, you have to address what you have perceived for so long as brokenness, and embrace it. You have lived a life worth sharing with others, but remember, you can't love others big until you love yourself big. What memories or wrongs have you refused to let go? Make a list of the things that have dragged you down. This could be a foreclosed dream house, being fired from a great job, or an injury that took away your ability to do things you once did. Write that list, and one by one feel those feelings, then think of ways you can flip these and do some good. If you broke your leg and can't run the same, can you sponsor someone in a charity walk? If you were let go from a job you loved, can you volunteer somewhere in a similar capacity? Brainstorm ways that you could take the hurts and turn those feelings into empathy that helps you to support others.

**Day Seven:** The heart has the ability to beat more than 3 billion times in a person's life. For you to find more hope to live a fuller life, it's key that you make your heart beat with purpose. Speak life into your soul today. Go to the nearest mirror and say some positive things that directly contradict any unkind words that have been spoken over you before. If you had a classmate call you ugly as a child and you've carried that with you, speak beauty over your soul. If you had a bad breakup and they told you that you were nothing but full of baggage, give yourself a pep talk and tell your soul that you have a life that is lovely with a big, beautiful mess.

So here we are at the end of Week 2. I hope your puppy is wagging its tail, wanting more. Taking care of your heart is so extremely important. Feel all the feels, get squishing with it, cha-cha with it, shield it when necessary, let your tribe hug it—just don't let it drive the bus! And now with our mind and body detoxed, we turn our attention to our body. In the next chapter, I will not be offering you the latest diet fad or suggesting a certain exercise routine. Detoxing your body is truly about shifting your relationship with it...and caring for it from the inside out.

# Week 3

## Detoxing the Body

> "We are not human beings in search of a spiritual experience. We are spiritual beings immersed in a human experience."
>
> **—Wayne Dyer**

The human body is extraordinary!

Think about it. Mature bodies create more bodies. Baby bodies that begin less than ten pounds (in most cases) become fully formed in less than two decades. Sick bodies can receive transplants, and heal, and live. Dead bodies can donate parts and keep other countless bodies alive and even help them heal. Isn't that just mind-boggling when you think about it? Our body is growing hair while shedding it along with dead skin cells. All the while, it is regenerating, making more than 3.8 million cells every single second.[31] Nearly all of those cells are blood cells, and our bodies pump more than 2,000 gallons of blood through the heart more than 100,000 times a day.[32]

The human body does so many things automatically, without our brains telling it to. Our eyes process visual signals, then blink, and then the electrical signals travel to the brain where billions of neurons process these signals and make meaning of it all.[33] The body runs like a super-computer, and yet every single atom is made of stardust and is billions of years old.[34]

Every time I think I might be taking my mystical, energetic body                                    ite:

31  Michelle Star, "Your Body Makes 3.8 Million Cells Every Second. Most of Them Are Blood," Science Alert, January 23, 2021, https://www.sciencealert.com/your-body-makes-4-million-cells-a-second-and-most-of-them-are-blood.

32  Nectarsleep Editorial Team, "90 Fun & Weird Facts About The Human Body," Nectar, Updated August 16, 2022, https://www.nectarsleep.com/posts/fun-facts-about-the-human-body/.

33  Claire Nowak, "15 Incredible Things the Human Body Does Every Minute," The Healthy, March 4, 2018, https://www.thehealthy.com/bodies/human-body-every-minute/.

34  Brian Clegg, "20 Amazing Facts About the Human Body," The Guardian, January 26, 2013, https://www.theguardian.com/science/2013/jan/27/20-human-body-facts-science.

It catalogs what our bodies do each second, and it's incredible to see the tallies tick up as our bodies work their magic.

So, it's no wonder that when we fail to honor the body, it negatively affects us on all levels (mind, body, heart, soul). Failing to take care of your body gets you in a funk that is so very hard to get out of, but so worth it when you do. The first step to honoring our bodies is becoming more aware of what the body needs. And the second step is acknowledging those needs without judgment and not letting any outside influence determine what your body needs. It's *your* body. You know what it needs—once you're better tuned in to it—and that is your goal for this week.

## WHAT IS YOUR BODY?

"The atoms of our bodies are traceable to stars that manufactured them in their cores and exploded these enriched ingredients across our galaxy, billions of years ago. For this reason, we are biologically connected to every other living thing in the world. We are chemically connected to all molecules on Earth. And we are atomically connected to all atoms in the universe. We are not figuratively, but literally stardust."

**—Neil deGrasse Tyson**

Well, it's our vessel, our mode of transportation, keeper of our soul, wardrobe of our heart and mind. The body is the catalyst for physically moving within the universe. Bodies are also the way in which we tangibly present ourselves to others within the world. But bodies are so much more than that.

We literally have the universe within us! Think I'm crazy? I'm not. We are made of stardust.[35]

"[A] new survey of 150,000 stars shows just how true the old cliché is: Humans and their galaxy have about 97 percent of the same kind of atoms" according to space. com.[36] Interestingly enough, the human brain atoms look a lot like the universe atoms under a microscope,[37] which may seem like unimportant trivia to some, but to me, I totally geek out over this stuff.

The fact that the universe is within us is proof that we are all connected as beings to each other, to the Earth, to everything all around us. We are all made up of the same substance. Microscopically, everything is energy. And since energy cannot be created or destroyed, we are not just the universe, but eternal!

This microscopic revelation is essentially a manifestation of our magic. If we are full of energy, we should

---

35 Simon Worrall, "How 40,000 Tons of Cosmic Dust Falling to Earth Affects You and Me," *National Geographic,* January 28, 2015, https://www.nationalgeographic.com/news/2015/01/150128-big-bang-universe-supernova-astrophysics-health-space-ngbooktalk/.

36 Elizabeth Howell, "Humans Really Are Made of Stardust, and a New Study Proves It," Space, January 10, 2017, https://www.space.com/35276-humans-made-of-stardust-galaxy-life-elements.html.

37 Tim Childers, "The Human Brain Looks Suspiciously Like the Universe, Which May Freak You Out," *Popular Mechanics,* November 17, 2020, https://www.popularmechanics.com/science/a34703841/human-brain-universe-similarities/.

make the most of our time on Earth. Our spirits are bursting with energy, ready to embrace life with passion... but our bodies are often too tired and worn down to allow this personal Supernova. This is why a body detox is crucial. By "body detox" I don't mean the typical LOSE TEN POUNDS by the dieting industry spamming you with ads. I mean a new way of relating to your body so that it becomes a clean and clear canvas for the universe to move through you.

## HOW DO WE RELATE TO OUR BODY?

> "The body often contains emotional truths that words can too easily gloss over."
>
> **—Esther Perel**

We have to reckon with our bodies each day. We live within them! Every day, we ponder things like, what do we feel like, look like, or work like? What is our strength level, emotional state, and our confidence level? These beliefs we have about ourselves affect not only how we feel toward ourselves, but how we interact with others.

These thoughts about our bodies, if left to run wild, can begin to dictate our behaviors and activities. We can easily become overly occupied with our clothes and accessories, workout regimen, or even the belongings that support our wellbeing—like kitchen gadgets and workout machines or the latest health monitoring device—instead of paying attention to our bodies.

This preoccupation with things can take the place of time that could be better spent with those whom we love enjoying shared activities with, or alone in peaceful solidarity: meditating, exercising, or taking nature walks. It's about balance—bodies are important for many reasons, but our bodies are not the most important thing about us and our existence on this planet.

There are two very different ways of relating to the body. One is external and dependent on others approval, judgment, and rating, and the other is all about honoring our bodies regardless of any external influences.

Statistically, in 2020, healthcare spending in the US reached $4.1 trillion, or $12,530 per person, and accounted for 19.7 percent of gross domestic product (GDP).[38] For those of us who spend money on beauty and fitness, we spend around $3,000–$4,000 a year on it and, staggeringly, around $200,000 during our lifetimes cumulatively![39]

These self-care expenditures can be wonderful things, as long as the motivation is *not* external. If we continue to lack the self-love that is needed, then our efforts and expenses are misguided! Our motivation should be to be our best, shiniest, loveliest version of ourselves, for ourselves, first and foremost.

Because think about it: without our bodies, we are nothing. Even achieving a higher consciousness can't

---

38   "NHE Fact Sheet," Centers for Medicare & Medicaid Services, accessed November 16, 2022, https://www.cms.gov/Research-Statistics-Data-and-Systems/Statistics-Trends-and-Reports/National-HealthExpendData/NHE-Fact-Sheet.

39   "The Real Price of Beauty in the US," Booksy, February 4, 2020, https://booksy.com/blog/us/the-real-price-of-beauty-in-the-us/#:~:text=Among%20those%20who%20regularly%20invest,reports%20the%20New%20York%20Post.

happen without being attached permanently to a body. The only way we get to experience this world and our life is through the vessel that carries us. Much like the cars, trains and planes that transport us from one place to another, and we need to take very good care of our vessel.

Our bodies are miracles and deserve our respect and awe. Just as we look at a beautiful, picturesque landscape flanked by a starry sky and take a moment to admire it, we should do the same with our amazing bodies.

The body we dwell within is so complex, it's not even fully understood by those that have spent their lifetimes studying it. Gaining a basic knowledge of our human biology can help us understand the importance of caring for the body.[40] The body is magical, and it is mysterious. Our true self is reliant on the healthiest version of our body. Without it, we can't travel through our lives and this world. It's our vehicle...and like any good engine, it needs to run, and be tended to and cared for.

## MINDING OUR BODIES

So, what does it mean to mind our body? It means becoming mindful of it and aligning with it. We will dive into mindfulness and meditation in Week 5, but in short, mindfulness is part of the progression toward raising our awareness of our bodies—and focusing on what we are feeling, seeing, and experiencing without judgment, that

---

40   Allison Sadlier, SWNS, "Most people barely know anything about the human body," *New York Post*, June 24, 2020, https://nypost.com/2020/06/24/how-much-do-people-actually-know-about-the-human-body/.

very moment.[41] Mindfulness is a vital step in becoming more aware of what our bodies need.

One of the very first things the majority of meditation teachers do is to make you very, very aware of your body and your breath. So, meditation isn't transcending the body, it is inviting the universe in. And our bodies welcome this when we allow them to, because we are inextricably connected.

The first time I tried to meditate, one of the biggest issues I had was that it completely hurt my back. I was really envious of people who could sit in a full lotus (padmasana) position for long periods of time. Because of the pain I was in, I was horribly fidgety. Eventually, I learned to sink into my body and accept my physical form while letting my thoughts go and staying in the present moment. When I paid attention to my pain, and concentrated on it, I found the back pain would go away. Eventually I learned how to meditate without fidgeting, even if I had to adjust and use my own unique positions.

Our bodies deserve and *need* our attention. True mindfulness or awareness cannot be achieved without coming to peace and partnership with our bodies. We live in our bodies, and we need to be mindful of what they need.

---

41    Mayo Clinic Staff, "Mindfulness exercises," Mayo Clinic, accessed November 16, 2022, https://www.mayoclinic.org/healthy-lifestyle/consumer-health/in-depth/mindfulness-exercises/art-20046356#:~:-text=Mindfulness%20is%20a%20type%20of,mind%20and%20help%20reduce%20stress.

# SHIFTING OUR RELATIONSHIP WITH OUR BODIES

> "A woman watches her body uneasily, as though it were an unreliable ally in the battle for love."
>
> **—Leonard Cohen**

We now agree that human thoughts by default tend to lean toward the negative (Week 1) and our thoughts about our body are no exception, if we're not intentional. So, as we retrain our brains to choose positive thoughts—we must also alter our internal view of ourselves.

Your body is a very needed part of this journey, so please don't ignore it, obsess about it externally to please others, or forget that it is the container of your spirit.

The stories we tell ourselves about our bodies are often cruel.

Body image is how you view yourself when you either envision yourself in your mind, or actually look at yourself in the mirror.[42] It also includes how we *think* others see us. This very closely relates to our self-image, "The idea one has of one's abilities, appearance, and personality," according to the dictionary definition. In either case, it's made up. It is not factual information. And it is defined by you and your view. Every day you can determine whether you are a beautiful goddess/god with magical abilities or not.

---

42  "Body Image," National Eating Disorders Association, accessed November 16, 2022, https://www.nationaleatingdisorders.org/body-image-0.

We alone calculate our labels and our worth. Our identity—our memories, experiences, relationships, and the values that we create in our mind according to our circumstances[43]—is so closely related to our worth. We are in control of our worth. As a result, we cannot place all of our identity and self-worth on our external image. It is like a photograph—it is a snapshot of who we are. It is not the wholeness of who we are.

If you view yourself as beautiful, despite any physical appearance details, then that will give you self-confidence—the feeling of trust that you are capable, have good qualities, and have the ability to contribute.[44] We can't tie beauty to youth or a particular look—we have to associate it with our body, which in and of itself is a walking miracle. Otherwise, as we age or our bodies "fail," we will question our worth.

Living a life that is healthy, full, and productive is contingent on our self-image being positive and having a good working relationship with our bodies, no matter our actual physical abilities. We have to choose to see our bodies as a catalyst for our mind, soul, heart, and our connection to our creator and Earth, not an object to be revered or disregarded.

43   "Body Image," *Psychology Today*, accessed November 16, 2022 https://www.psychologytoday.com/us/basics/identity.

44   Mind Tools Content Team, "How to Build Self-Confidence," MindTools, accessed November 16, 2022, https://www.mindtools.com/self-conf.html.

> "The body we see within the collection of arms and legs is simply a hallucination of our ignorant mind."
>
> **—Kelsang Gyatso**

We all have different bodies, but that doesn't mean that we should all have different body image issues. We can decide that each body is worthy of praise. Because every single individual body blesses the world, albeit differently, but always equally. We all have the choice to either dwell on what's wrong with our bodies and subsequently potentially develop unhealthy habits, or we can all choose to love our bodies, despite differences, because all bodies are moving miracles.

We choose to either have a body image that is healthy or one that isn't. Just as we choose how to view the world externally, we must choose how we view ourselves. I've tried it both ways, and trust me, I would choose to view body positively, to the best of my abilities, every single time. Because how we view ourselves determines much of what we do, say, feel, and act throughout our entire lives.

Self-care can't happen unless we first have a healthy view of ourselves. A warped self-image can often lead to low self-worth, which can then lead to—in some cases—self-harm.

When I entered college years ago, I had some "baby fat" already, and after a couple semesters of partying and not taking care of my health, I became borderline anorexic. Sometime in my mid-twenties, I promised myself that I would never diet.

I didn't like my "baby fat" or want this state of mind and being, but I also knew that I didn't want to get into the endless cycle of dieting that many women fall into. So, I made the declaration that no matter how much weight I gained, I would not go on a diet or weigh myself unless I absolutely needed to.

That decision alone has helped me maintain my weight within a fifteen-pound window for a few decades. And I plan to keep that vow. Our bodies give us so much, we should honor and cherish them, no matter what happens: loss of mobility, weight gain, or cancer.

## THE BODY AS SPIRITUAL PATH

"We are not human beings having a spiritual experience. We are spiritual beings having a human experience."

**—Pierre Teilhard de Chardin**

Is the body to be viewed as divine? Like a temple? Or a sin-ridden, corrupt vessel that traps and pollutes the Holy Spirit inside us? As you go on this spiritual path, it's important to ponder this question. I am, again, on Team Magical Beings. Because...we are made of stardust.

Your meditation and exercise should first and foremost be ways for you to be in control of your life and write your story. Not ways to torture your body. This world does enough of that. You need not be your own worst critic and punisher!

The thing that has to be underscored the most about the body is that it is not our identity. It holds our identity. It is the keeper of our soul, our mind, and heart. It is our connection to the Earth, our Higher Power, and our vessel to move about and bless the Earth with our creativity and love.

Our thoughts, words, and actions in our lives must be in alignment for our lives to "be."

Buddha was neutral on whether or not the body is bad or good. Rather, he emphasized the need to harness mindfulness and awareness of the body to discover the dharma, the truth of how things are. The Buddha saw our bodies as vehicles to enable us to reach full consciousness and fully understand our place in reality, and thus find our real path—our True North. In Christianity, the body is a sacred temple for the Holy Spirit, and can be damaged by sin or saved by God. In Judaism, the body is made in God's image and therefore to be respected and honored. Whether you believe the body can perform miracles, or if you have a more scientific perspective on the human form, the point is, our body is our only vehicle given to us in this life. All religions agree in one way or another that the body is a sacred vessel that can carry our consciousness forward, and needs to be honored.

## SELF-CARE ISN'T SELFISHNESS

I've had sciatica since I was twenty-four, and it is mostly manageable, but I still have flare ups. Sciatica is pain that moves along the sciatic nerve, which spans the whole lower portion of your body.[45] Typically, sciatica affects only one side of your body. The worst flare up I had was when I had a young baby that needed to be held.

When my son was eight months old, my back gave out completely. Worst timing ever, and it really messed with my self-worth and my view of myself as a new mother. I went to change his diaper in the middle of the night, and as I picked him up from his crib and put him on the changing table, my knees completely buckled. I was on the floor. Thankfully I was able to sit him down gently before I went down.

My partner at the time had earplugs in so she could not hear me. We lived in a big Victorian home, and I had to inch my way to her on the floor, while calling out. Mind you, my son was still on the changing table unattended, and by then, crying uncontrollably.

My partner at the time finally heard us and came running in to help. It took her and her best friend (who she called and who sped over) nearly two hours to get me into the car, so we could go to the emergency room.

When the doctor saw me, he said, "I will be giving you narcotics to ease you to sleep." This was because the pain was so excruciating; I was writhing in pain, screaming. A very long story short, I was unable to move for six weeks after. I was a fixture in the furniture.

I would say that I was bedridden, but I couldn't even sleep on my back. I would fall asleep face down with propped up on pillows under my stomach (imagine a cow or horse sleeping upright). This was for six whole weeks.

---

45   Mayo Clinic, "Sciatica," https://www.mayoclinic.org/diseases-con-ditions/sciatica/symptoms-causes/syc-20377435#:~:text=Sciatica%20 refers%20to%20pain%20that,one%20side%20of%20your%20body.

Two months of my baby's new life, practically. Not only was it extremely frustrating, but it was also embarrassing and heartbreaking, as it was the first time that I could not hold my son.

Up until then, my body would tag along with whatever I decided to do. I would overwork it, be exhausted, deprive it of sleep, forget to eat, drink a little too much, etc.

But the night my back completely went out while holding my baby, I knew that I couldn't keep pushing my body. Me: 0. Body: 1. The baby needed me. My body was no longer functioning as it should. It became very evident to me right away that without my body, I could do nothing.

Though I could not move, I was still worthy. I could still think, talk, sing, and soothe my baby. I could still observe, practice mindfulness. I decided then that I would never completely take my body for granted again.

We all intuitively know we should take good care of our bodies, but we often fall short of doing so. Why? Because life is busy. But we find out all too quickly that if we don't make self-love a priority, we will fall prey to putting ourselves last on the list. In the business of life, we tend to take our bodies, our vessels, for granted—until something goes wrong with it and we are forced to contend with tending to our body's needs.

## CURATE YOUR SELF-LOVE

There are thousands of books on how to take care of ourselves and plenty of influencers on social media, TV, and radio listing all of the ways we can take better care of ourselves. In truth, there is no one-size-fits all approach to self-love—like there is no other you. For the self-help junkies out there, how many times have you read about the best way to treat your body, the best way to be in a relationship, the best way to meditate, etc....and yet it hasn't worked for you, or hasn't worked for you for very long? I remember speaking with a colleague and I said that in the early days of my breakup, it was my family and friends who were my lifeline. She said that was interesting because her way of healing was to isolate herself, to take a step back from everything and everyone in order to reset. While I can completely appreciate her process and she mine, we clearly have different paths to healing and well-being. Our bodies are no different. There's a woman in my outer circle who goes trail running for ten to fifteen miles almost daily. You couldn't pay me enough to do so. I could run a mile—maybe. It's simply not my jam. But I feel I can swim forever. So why would I spend time trying to run miles I don't want to do—which doesn't resonate with me—when I can figure out how to incorporate swimming and walking—two activities that make me feel alive—into my everyday...or every other day?

There are, however, some basic truths we all share. We all need sleep, we all need to breathe, we all need to eat—and eat well—and we all need to take care of our bodies and (physical) hearts with some form of activity/exercise.

Some of us are better or worse at eating well, sleeping, exercising, and limiting alcohol and drug (prescription and recreational) intakes. All of these are extremely important to our health and well-being, and once we have a clear understanding of why the body is so extremely important in the mind/heart/body trifecta, none of them will feel like a chore...because they become part of your personal Supernova.

# THE IMPORTANCE OF SLEEP

According to a recent Gallup poll, nearly half of all American adults (40 percent) are sleep-deprived, sleeping a lot less than the daily recommended amount of seven hours of sleep per night.

Arianna Huffington is co-founder and editor in chief of The Huffington Post and is also a sleep guru. In her book *The Sleep Revolution: Transforming Your Life, One Night at a Time*[46], she reveals how the cultural view of sleep as time wasted is not only a misnomer but horribly wrong.

This misguided belief that sleep is not an important part of our life leads to poor decision-making, health issues, poor performance in our personal (sex) and professional (career) lives. Sleep, and restful sleep at that, is arguably one of the most important forms of self-love we can give ourselves each and every day.

How ironic that half of us are not getting enough sleep, because a big chunk (33 percent) of our life is spent sleeping![47]

It's proven that getting behind the wheel of a moving vehicle without adequate sleep is just as dangerous as getting drunk then driving.[48] Not sleeping enough is truly dangerous, not just for you, but those around you. You can essentially sleepwalk through life if you aren't more intentional about your sleep cycle.

---

46  "The Sleep Revolution," WordPress, accessed November 16, 2022, https://www.ariannahuffington.com/the-sleep-revolution/.

47  Michael J. Aminoff et al., "We spend about one-third of our life either sleeping or attempting to do so," *National Library of Medicine,* 2011;98:vii. Doi: 10.1016/B978-0-444-52006-7.00047-2, accessed November 16, 2022, https://pubmed.ncbi.nlm.nih.gov/21056174/.

48  Danielle Pacheco, "Drowsy Driving vs. Drunk Driving: How Similar Are They?," Sleep Foundation, June 24, 2022, https://www.sleepfoundation.org/drowsy-driving/drowsy-driving-vs-drunk-driving.

When we enter into a restful sleep, we get more energized. This can serve as a catalyst to launch you into being a more powerful person each day. Instead of crashing and burning, you can burst out of bed with energy. Sleep is so vital to every part of our existence, and lack of it can cause a plethora of illnesses!

Sleep is something we all have to do, but we may not know how to do it well. Improving sleep quality is a process, but the good news is that you can get your sleep path on the right track, starting tonight. It takes know-how and follow through, just like most beneficial things in life. To avoid sleep disruptions, try doing the following:[49]

1. **Get a doctor's professional opinion for hot flashes or feelings of being tired while awake.** These can happen because of hormonal imbalances or even obstructive sleep apnea, and can be treated in a number of ways. The only way to know is for a professional to check you out.

2. **Start a sleep schedule.** Start resting and getting up at the same time each day. Restful rhythms happen when your body's circadian rhythm is in sync (the natural, internal process that regulates the sleep-wake cycle and repeats on each rotation of the Earth roughly every twenty-four hours).[50]

---

49  "In search of sleep," *Women's Health*, Harvard Health Publishing, June 1, 2020, https://www.health.harvard.edu/womens-health/in-search-of-sleep.

50  Natalie Silver, "Everything to Know About Your Circadian Rhythm," Healthline, Updated March 30, 2022, https://www.healthline.com/health/healthy-sleep/circadian-rhythm#:~:text=Your%20circadian%20rhythm%20helps%20control,as%20well%20as%20other%20factors.

3. **Skip later-in-the-day caffeinated or alcoholic drinks.** These substances can disrupt your restful sleep.

4. **Skip staring at blue screens late at night.** Screens have blue light emitted directly at your eyes, so shutting off phones or keeping them out of your bedroom for at least an hour before you plan to sleep is a good idea. Try meditating, reading, or other non-electronic activities before sleeping.

5. **Exercise earlier in the day, not before bed.** Working out later in the day can actually be less beneficial for your sleep patterns because exercise can be stimulating.

6. **Create a tranquil sanctuary.** Aim for a quiet, cool, dark room.

This is hard to do at first, but the benefits we see from more restful sleep make our emotional, mental, physical state so worth it. It's not really a sacrifice to unplug, because unplugging is how we recharge.

We wouldn't expect a machine to keep plugging along without ever getting recharged, so why would we expect our very organic bodies to keep going without recharging by resting? The same goes for how we eat. We can't eat food that doesn't energize us and expect to feel full of energy.

We spend far more time worrying about what we look like externally. And even when we diet and exercise, it is because we want to look better externally rather than acknowledging, nurturing, and honoring the body because it is our holy vessel.

## CHOOSING SOUL FOOD, NOT JUNK FOOD

The old proverbial saying "You are what you eat" rings true when choosing to consider food more than just mere fuel to make your body move; if you consider food to be "soul food," then it really can empower your body, mind, heart, and soul, just as soul music does.

Soul food can both comfort your essence and represent your true self. Just as the original meaning of soul food has been used to refer to food that is sort of down-home cooking with roots in the deep south and African American cuisine, soul food can also refer to any food that you consume that makes your soul sing.

How can a substance that we consume do all of those things? How can food bring life to our being? Because you have both a physical body and a spiritual body, your soul. Both need to be fed!

According to Eckhart Tolle, the choices that people make can be connected to their spirituality and more specifically Ahimsa.[51] Ahimsa, in the Hindu, Buddhist, and Jainist traditions, essentially means respect for all living things and avoidance of violence toward others.[52]

You are a unique being, and the food you eat should be individualized as well. It's scientific. Everyone has different fingerprints,[53] and everyone has different taste

---

51    Eckhart Tolle, "What Is the Relationship Between Diet & Spirituality?," YouTube video, 4:39, May 2, 2019, https://youtu.be/BZ8LXmp-FEFw.

52    Sejal Shah, "What is Ahimsa? All You Need to Know to Learn the Art of Non-Violence," The Art of Living, Updated July 28, 2020, https://www.artofliving.org/us-en/non-violence-and-the-art-of-ahimsa.

53    "Why do people have different fingerprints?," Washington State University, accessed November 16, 2022, https://askdruniverse.wsu.edu/2020/02/07/people-different-fingerprints/#:~:text=Everyone's%20skin%20grows%20in%20a,are%20covered%20in%20friction%20ridges.

buds.[54] The reason for the variance in the different finger-prints is that everyone's body grows skin at different rates, because we all live in different environments. The cause for the varying tastebud collections is because everyone has a different genetic makeup and thus cell compilation in their mouths.

Tolle insists that it's most important to be present while eating, reaching down deep and asking what your soul needs to be nourished, for the food to be converted to true soul energy.

So then, your state of mind determines what you need, but again, remember the mind is demanding. If you felt super great eating an entire tub of ice cream after a breakup, you may reach for that same container to feel a similar release.

Likewise, if your mind remembers that a fresh green salad sourced from local ingredients made you feel like a million bucks, you might make that for yourself when your mammogram comes back free and clear, celebrating the miracle of healthy breast tissue cells. It is all about reaching your own decision, determining what you need for nourishment at the moment.

Being in tune with what your body wants and needs is key here. It is either a spiritual dilemma you must face daily, weekly, monthly, yearly, for the entirety of your life, or it is a practice that you engage with regularly. The awareness within your mind allows you to know and *feel* what you need.

---

54   "Why Are Everyone's Tastebuds Different?," SiOWfa 15: Science in Our World; Certainty and Controversy, WordPress, accessed November 16, 2022, https://sites.psu.edu/siowfa15/2015/10/22/why-are-every-ones-taste-buds-different/.

What you need now may differ from what you needed when you were younger or as you age. As you change, your needs change. Different seasons of life demand different nourishment, and practicing that discipline of being in tune with what your being needs will ensure that you are satisfied as you go through the different seasons.

Everyone is on a different spiritual path, so everyone has different soul food needs. Each person has different sensitivities, allergies, and as we discussed, different taste buds. And this is not a diet book. So, I will refrain from listing the many healthy or indulgent (or a mix of both) options you could select. That would take me volumes of books. I will, however, list a few enlightening soul offerings that can benefit any human being, despite their background, age, beliefs, or current mood.

## Soul-Giving Foods

- Raw fruits and vegetables

- Cooked vegan food

- Organic, clean grass-fed livestock

- Grains and legumes

- Survival foods—non-perishables (low in sodium and sugar)

From time to time, you may need to consume and do some things for your nutritional needs that don't necessarily coincide with the aforementioned. And these items are on far ends of a spectrum—I'm talking about indulging in junk food and endeavoring a cleanse.

I know, I know. We've talked a lot about soul food and giving your body what it needs. Sometimes, your body really does need a holiday sweet treat. And other times, your body needs a cleanse. On either occasion, you will have discretionary control over which is necessary at the time.

Some foods keep us rooted firmly to the Earth, and in most cases this is not consuming other creatures. This is because metabolizing these foods costs us, sometimes not just physically but also morally.

Ultimately, it's a personal choice which foods fuel your body and soul. It's transactional, much like sleep. You must decide for yourself which foods give you more than what they take to consume and process. This process is about thriving, not just surviving on food.

## Fasting

We've covered a lot of ground when talking about food and our spiritual relationship with it. Arguably though, perhaps the best way to fully be connected to the universe and realize your need to coexist peacefully with it is to fast, also known as omitting food. There are many spiritual benefits when it comes to denying your body food. This is not an expression of vanity. This is not an attempt to lose physical weight, rather this is an attempt to shed the weight of worries and connections to nonessential, man-made constraints within your existence.

### Spiritual benefits of fasting:

- Cleansing of the soul

- Deeper connection to the universe/Earth

- Deeper desire to know your Higher Power/God

- Increased ability to hear inner voice/know your soul needs

- Prolonged satisfaction—meeting needs beyond meeting immediate thirst/hunger

Fasting is not about suffering, but rather reaching a new level of awareness moving toward your truest self and increasing your vibration to the highest frequency (more on this when we cover True North).

## EXERCISE YOUR BODY, ENERGIZE YOUR SOUL

"Metabolism slows down 90 percent after 30 minutes of sitting. The enzymes that move the bad fat from your arteries to your muscles, where it can get burned off, slow down. And after two hours, good cholesterol drops 20 percent. Just getting up for five minutes is going to get things going again. These things are so simple they're almost stupid."

**—Gavin Bradley**

There is an undeniable connection between physical fitness and spirituality. The physical and spiritual parts of you are not at odds—these parts are both integral parts of your existence that deserve equal attention.

Our bodies are meant to move to the best of our abilities. Every time you move your body, you can think about all of the aches and pains you have. Or every time that you move, you can be thankful that your body moves. Your motivation should be to keep your body healthy, moving along to the rhythm of your vibration frequency.

Flexibility in mind and body is part of the ultimate spiritual maturity level. Flexibility of the body relates to the ability a person has to move their body using their joints, muscles, and balance.[55] Mind (cognitive) flexibility refers to the ability to switch between thinking about two different concepts or to think about multiple concepts simultaneously.[56]

I mention both because as you take control of your mind, give your heart a big squeeze, and begin to love your body big, you will be able to move the energy within your body more freely. You may not be able to bend like you used to, but you can still connect to the Earth and feel the energy flow. It's about gratitude and going with the flow of your body.

As you seek to improve your flexibility on both levels, ponder how you can continue to stretch yourself both physically and spiritually. This will keep your mind and body in alignment. Here are some ways to keep your mind and body flexible:

- Deep breathing exercises

- Yoga

- Pilates

55  Sports Medicine, "Flexibility," UC Davis Health, https://health.uc-davis.edu/sports-medicine/resources/flexibility.
56  K.R. Magnusson, B.L. Brim, "The Aging Brain," *Reference Module in Biometric Sciences,* ScienceDirect, 2014, https://www.sciencedirect.com/topics/neuroscience/cognitive-flexibility#:~:text=Cognitive%20flexibility%20refers%20to%20the,think%20about%20multiple%20concepts%20simultaneously.

- Dance

- Warm bath

By building a firm foundation of flexibility with your body's ability, it's a good idea to explore some more rigorous exercise activities. This will not only really get your body moving, but it will also get your heart pumping and endorphins increasing. Endorphins are essentially a natural high that your body gives itself when you move, primarily to help you cope with stress while minimizing the effects of pain.[57] A more positive mindset is achieved with the release of tension and stress. More rigorous exercises may include:

- Endurance/aerobic (swimming, dancing, jogging, biking, climbing, tennis, etc.)

- Strength or weight training (squats, planks, lifting weights, push-ups, pull-ups, etc.)

Committing to enduring rigorous exercise makes you appreciate the processes of your body—heart pumping, breathing cycles, joint/muscle movement—and your connection and reliance on the Earth and its gravity and elements. Becoming stronger makes you appreciate all that your body can do. It helps you reach a rhythm of body and Earth synergy that increases your vibration, deepens your awareness, and ultimately connects you to your Higher Power on the deepest level.

---

57 Katy Davidson, MScFN, RD, CPT, "Why Do We Need Endorphins?," Healthline, Updated November 30, 2021, https://www.healthline.com/health/endorphins#:~:text=Endorphins%20are%20polypeptides%20made%20by,occurs%20due%20to%20endorphin%20activity.

The short- and long-term benefits of exercise are possibly immeasurable. The most immediate benefit of exercising in an effort to increase your flexibility, strength, and endurance is a greater sense of motivation. And the most persistent benefit is actually the potential to make your brain sharper and even increase your lifespan.[58]

Putting your body into motion can be a time for you to reflect on your thought patterns and behaviors and to release your tension as you give yourself more time to become more aware of your needs. As you engage in repetitive, intentional movement, your brain can slow down enough to become more present in the moment and move your awareness around freely. I have had major breakthroughs while hiking in nature. I know this is a common occurrence; by testing will, endurance, and carving out time for yourself to move your body, you can finally see truths that you may not have acknowledged prior.

When you look inside yourself and see how strong you really are through physical activity, your mind becomes quieter, and the soul is energized.

## Breathe!!!!

How often do you find yourself holding your breath? I do it all the time. Sometimes so much so that I am surprised I am still alive. Even now, I have to remind myself to breathe. It's interesting how much we ignore the very thing that we all need and can easily access and guide to our benefit. What's worse is that when we're stressed, we often take

---

58   Kalia Kelmenson, "The Hidden Benefits of Exercise," Spirituality&Health, accessed November 16, 2022, https://www.spirituality-health.com/blogs/the-present-moment/2019/01/14/the-hidden-benefits-of-exercise.

short shallow breaths from the chest. This type of thoracic breathing actually adds to our anxiety and can increase the heart rate, contribute to dizziness, create muscle tension, and other physical ailments because our blood is not being properly oxygenated. However, deep breathing (also known as diaphragmatic breathing) helps regulate our blood flow, heart rate and digestion.

Breathing is extremely powerful and mostly underrated. There have been multiple studies on the positive effects of breathing exercises and breathwork on our bodies and mental health.[59] Breathing is our body's natural way of constantly detoxing—oxygen in, carbon dioxide out. Breathing exercises and breathwork can differ depending on intention. While some breathing exercises can help you relax and ease anxiety and worry, other breathing exercises can help you focus and feel energized. Breathwork is a term used to describe any type of therapy that utilizes breathing exercises to improve physical, mental, emotional, and spiritual health. It can be a very emotional experience. There have been quite a few times where I have sobbed throughout my breathwork. It feels deep, visceral, and primal...as if I am breathing my ancestor's breaths and that my breaths connect me to all other beings. It's gorgeous, powerful, heartbreaking, and ultimately liberating. Let's take a look at both breathing exercises and breathwork.

---

59   Bruce Goldman, "Study shows slow breathing induces tranquility," Stanford Medicine, March 30, 2017, https://med.stanford.edu/news/all-news/2017/03/study-discovers-how-slow-breathing-induces-tranquility.html.

## Breathing Exercises

You're probably asking yourself, "How hard is it to breathe?!" Much like meditation, it is not hard to do at all but the more you practice, the greater the benefits. Here's a partial list of breathing exercises. It's worth trying all of them to see what works best for you.

### Simple Breathing Exercise

This exercise can be done as often as you like whether standing, sitting, or lying down.

1. Make your body as relaxed as possible. Inhale slowly and deeply through your nose. Don't force anything.

2. Exhale slowly through your mouth. You can purse your lips a bit but be sure to keep your mouth and jaw relaxed.

3. Repeat the inhaling and exhaling for several minutes until you feel very relaxed.

### Diaphragmatic (Belly) Breathing

I've found belly breathing to be one of the fastest ways of relaxing. You can do it once a day for as little as a few minutes or up to ten minutes several times throughout the day.

Please do this exercise in whatever position that makes you feel most comfortable.

1. Place one hand on your upper chest and the other hand on your stomach.

2. Make sure your belly is relaxed, not tightened.

3. Breathe in slowly through your nose and downward toward your stomach so you can feel your belly rise and fall.

4. Exhale slowly through your mouth, making sure your jaw is relaxed. The hand on your chest may feel your heartbeat but it should not rise and fall like the hand on your belly. The breath should only come from your belly, not your chest.

## Pursed-Lip Breathing

Pursed-Lip Breathing is a great way of controlling oxygenation and ventilation. It's especially helpful for those who suffer from asthma or shortness of breath.

1. Sit comfortably and relax your neck and shoulder muscles.

2. Breathe in through your nose for two seconds while keeping your mouth closed. It doesn't need to be a deep breath.

3. Purse your lips as if you're going to blow out a candle.

4. Breathe out slowly through your pursed lips while counting down—four, three, two, one.

You're welcome to do this breath exercise four to five times a day.

## Alternate-Nostril Breathing (Nadi Shodhana)

Alternate-Nostril Breathing has become fairly popular in meditations and yoga and involves blocking off one nostril at a time as you breathe through the other, alternating between nostrils in a regular pattern.

1. Sit in a comfortable position with your back straight. Close your eyes.

2. Bring your right hand up to your nose and fold the index and middle fingers to the palm, so that you can use the thumb to close the right nostril, and the ring finger to close the left nostril.

3. Inhale and exhale to begin. Close off your right nostril with your thumb and inhale through your left nostril.

4. Close off your left nostril with your ring finger, then open and exhale through your right nostril.

5. Inhale through your right nostril, close off your right nostril with your thumb, then open and exhale through your left nostril. Now inhale through your left nostril.

6. Repeat this ten times.

Box Breathing

Box Breathing is super simple and frankly fun to do.

1. Exhale to a count of four.

2. Hold your breath for a count of four.

3. Inhale to a count of four.

4. Hold your breath for a count of four.

5. Exhale and start again.

Four-Seven-Eight Breathing

The Four-Seven-Eight Breathing exercise is quite popular as it instantly relaxes the nervous system. I've used it to help me sleep. If you're a beginner, please do the exercise sitting up with your back straight. Once you're familiar with the exercise, you can do it laying down.

1. Breathe into your belly and imagine filling up a balloon in your stomach.

2. Breathe in gently through your nose to a mental count of four.

3. Hold your breath to a count of seven.

4. Exhale through your mouth, making a whoosh sound to a count of eight.

5. Repeat and only focus on your breath.

## Lion's Breath (Simhasana)

Another popular breathing exercise, especially in yoga, is Lion's Breath. It is often used to release tension and become energized. Many refer to it as a "release valve" and it is an excellent way of purging. Whenever I do the Lion's Breath, I pretend I am Māori Warrior— fierce and powerful. It can also be silly and playful, depending on your mood.

1. Sit comfortably, close your eyes and take a few slow deep breaths. Some like to practice Lion's Breath sitting on their heels, with knees either together or apart. Fingers should be spread out and resting on your thighs or the floor.

2. Take a deep inhale through the nose, open your mouth as you exhale and stick your tongue out as far as possible down toward your chin. Stretch the muscles in your face while exhaling and make a "ha" sound that comes from deep within your belly. Your mouth should be as open as possible.

3. Repeat this 10 times.

The Lion's breath is an excellent way to let go of anger, frustrations, and upsets.

## Humming Bee Breathing (Bhramari)

I often like to hum when I meditate because it makes me feel like all my chakras are connected with the hum from the top of my head to my tailbone. I find the Humming Bee Breathing very soothing. It's also excellent for focus and concentration. I sometimes sway gently from side to side while sitting as the humming and movement make me feel like I'm seagrass in a gentle breeze. The swaying is just my thing. Add it if it feels right. Leave it out if it doesn't.

1. Sit comfortably, close your eyes and relax your body.

2. Place your index fingers on the cartilage between your cheek and ear (do not stick your fingers in your ear, just on the cartilage).

3. Take a deep breath in, and hum like a bee while exhaling and gently pressing the cartilage.

4. Continue to keep your eyes closed and feel the sensations in your body.

5. You can repeat this four to nine times.

Please note that if you have a lung condition or you're experiencing pain or difficulty with breathing, speak with a healthcare provider before trying any type of breathing exercise.

Breathwork

There are quite a few types of breathwork therapy, but most share the same foundation. Here is a partial list:

- Rebirthing Breathwork is also known as conscious energy breathing and its goal is to help release energy that has been blocked in our bodies and minds due to suppressed trauma. It was developed by Leonard Orr in the 1960s after what he claims to have been his own rebirth while sitting in a hot tub experimenting with deep breathing patterns. In treatment, participants are asked to lie down, relax, and breathe normally. Deep relaxation is used to prompt brain waves that lead to the release of subconscious issues and pent-up energy. Through the use of "conscious connected circular breathing" past traumas begin to surface and are often released. Sometimes participants are placed in an environment that resembles a womb and are guided through it. Another popular method involves submerging oneself in a bathtub and using a snorkel to stay underwater while breathing. The technique has been used to treat PTSD, depression, reactive attachment disorder, addiction, and more.

- Holotropic Breathwork was developed by psychiatrist Stanislov Grof in the 1970s as a drug-free way to induce altered states of consciousness. The intention of holotropic breathwork is to achieve oneness of mind, body, and spirit. Practitioners are trained and certified and often lead the sessions in groups.

Holotropic breathing involves lying down, relaxing, and breathing as rapidly and as deeply as possible. Once the holotropic breathing rhythm has been established, intense evocative music is played in combination with fast breathing, in order to induce a state of trance that allows for different levels of the unconscious to be reached. The length of a session depends on the individual and typically lasts between two and three hours. Sessions are often followed by discussion which help participants integrate what they have learned about themselves.

- Clarity Breathwork was developed by Ashanna Solaris and Dana DeLong (Dharma Devi). It's quite similar to rebirthing breathwork techniques. Clarity breathwork is based on the idea that most people do not breathe to their full capacity and its main goal is to teach people how to breathe fully. Therapy begins with an in-depth interview about present concerns and past experiences. Sessions include counseling, somatic exploration, and usually an hour of circular connected breathing practice. Clarity breathwork helps participants release stress and tension, heal unresolved trauma, gain deeper insights and access their internal healing energy, creativity, and greater awareness.

- Biodynamic Breathwork was created by Giten Tonkov and helps release chronic tension and emotional trauma through a six pillar approach to trauma integration; sound, touch, meditation, breath, emotional release and movement. Biodynamic breathwork recognizes trauma is stored psychologically and physically. Treatment sessions might incorporate exercises like deep, connected breathing and revisiting ingrained memories and sensations. It might also include music or sound therapy, vocalization, whole-body shaking, and even dance therapy.

- Shamanic breathwork may be my favorite. It is a healing process to awaken your true self. For thousands of years the shamans, also known as the medicine men and women, have used breath as a means to connect with the spirit world. Shamanic breathwork uses the breath, music, and movement as a tool to journey into expanded states. The belief is that we all have an inner shaman, an inner healer, who knows how to heal and transform. The Shamanic Breathwork technique involves breathing in through the nose and out through the mouth in a circular motion, which is one of the most powerful modalities for creating balance and harmony in our bodies. With every inhale, we increase our energy levels as we are breathing in the sacred life force. With every exhale our whole body relaxes as we release tension. The breathwork provides an opportunity for suppressed emotions to come to the surface and be released and serves as a gateway into the subconscious mind. Shamans believe that when we hold onto our emotions they can poison us, but when we allow them to freely move through our bodies, they can transform us. I wholeheartedly agree.

If you haven't done any work that involves your breath, please start with the breathing exercises and if you're so moved, try the breathwork. Both have been profound for me.

# DIS-EASE

I would be remiss if I didn't include a section on disease. Although it is our responsibility to take care of our bodies to the best of our abilities, disease happens, and we cannot spiritually bypass the fact. Sure, there are many spiritual, emotional, psychological, and nutritional tips and tricks to keep disease at bay, but disease can happen regardless. Guru Ram Dass had a debilitating stroke in 1997 at the age of sixty-six. Self-help author and motivational speaker Wayne Dyer was diagnosed with leukemia in 2009 and died of a heart attack in 2015 at the age of seventy-five. They were two of the most "woke" humans I know of, but all their transformation and spiritual transcendence did not make their diseases go away. They both came to accept their illnesses, and Ram Dass even considered it a gift, but the extent of their self-transformation had little bearing on their physical disease. Jeff Foster, one of my new favorite transformational speakers, suffered from Lyme disease for nearly two years at the age of forty. He did not know what he had for a good portion of it, and it took some time for him to recover from it. He has written considerably on the subject and what a challenge it was for him, not just physically but spiritually. It made him reevaluate everything he knew... or thought he knew.

Why do I mention them? To highlight the fact that while our mind, heart, and body work together, caring for one cannot be substituted for the other. Our bodies are our vessels through this life. We have to take care of them. Period. And if we are diagnosed with a disease, we have to do whatever possible to heal. While some may choose a holistic or ayurvedic approach, others may choose a more traditional medical path. No one can nor should they make that choice for you. What is most important is that you don't ignore the illness. And the sooner you can accept it, the sooner you'll be able to put your intentions for healing in motion.

During the writing of this book, my father had a major stroke, and my wife was diagnosed with cancer. The reality of disease took front and center. To ignore either would have been fatal. So, we embraced it. It was heartbreaking to witness my wife undergo chemo and radiation, though she did so gracefully. And for my father, a PhD professor of sixty years and celebrated architect, to go from a super-brain to excelled dementia within a day continues to boggle my mind and contract my heart. Disease is real. Accept it, embrace it, but don't let it determine your fate.

People who have life-limiting diseases often have existential and spiritual struggles as they face questions that have no easy answers. The seemingly endless challenges can be discouraging and exhausting. Understandably, some may begin to question beliefs that they have held throughout their lives. Much like going through other life struggles, there are breakthroughs beyond the breakdowns, and there are multiple ways of finding meaning and richness even through the hardest of times and the grief. No one chooses to be ill, but we can choose to rise in spite of it. Not easy, but doable and so very worth it.

> "Before the stroke, I was on a very spiritual plane. I ignored my body, took it for granted. When I look at my life, I see that I wanted to be free of the physical plane, the psychological plane, and when I got free of those, I didn't want to go anywhere near them. But the stroke reminded me that I had a body and a brain, that I had to honor them."
>
> **—Ram Dass**

# Week 3

## The Daily Purge

Remember, the Daily Purge is meant to be a brief block of time carved out of your busy day.

This week we are going to do the Daily Purge but by focusing exclusively on our bodies.

Even if you aren't going to do the daily exercises, please do the Daily Purge. It will help you shake off any weird feelings or thoughts you may have about your body. It will make you feel uplifted and refreshed. The minimum time you'll need is ten minutes, but twenty isn't the maximum either. Exercise as much as you see fit. This is all about intentionality and engagement. If you really want to get everything out of this book, then do the Daily Purge and the Daily Exercises.

# Week 3

## Exercise: Honoring Your Soul Vessel

**Day One:** Take an inventory of your body and how you see it. Reflect on your body image. How do you see yourself? Do you pay too much attention to how others see you? Or do you compare your body to others? What is your nutritional intake? What are your sleep patterns? What areas need further exploration in connection with your body, your diet, your exercise regimen, your sleep patterns? Make a one-page list as a reminder of the ways in which you are truly thankful for your body and all of its abilities.

**Day Two:** Take a walk with your body. Working with the body and beginning to accept one's own experience begins by paying close attention to what's happening in our experience of being human. Taking a positive attitude toward our bodies—being welcoming, accepting, and loving—begins with gratitude. As you walk, tell your body all the ways you are amazed by its abilities and make a promise to it that you will be the best steward you can be of the body that walks you through life.

**Day Three:** Get connected to nature through your senses. Listen to inspirational music or a podcast, or even just the sound of nature around you, and appreciate your ability to hear. If you are hearing impaired, focus on your eyes and the ability to see the beauty of the landscape. From there, practice mindfully paying attention to your surroundings, as you meander through nature. Ponder how the same atoms that your body is composed of are billions of years old and make up the universe. You are stardust. You are surrounded by stardust. You can also practice mindfulness by paying attention to how your body feels as you move through the world around you, feeling your senses. When your mind starts to wander, pull it back to the exercise without judging yourself. Bring your awareness back to how you feel as you move.

**Day Four:** Reflect on people who have loved your body in any way possible. As you move your body, imagine sending them positive energy and/

or prayers and gratitude for how they've loved you. See yourself through their eyes. If they ever turned around and hurt you, forgive them. Don't hold onto that tension or unforgiveness. It's toxic. Let your shoulders let go of that hurt. Don't let your body be burdened by any feelings of harboring hurt. Imagine the hurt being released.

**Day Five:** Meditate on a personal mantra or manifesto as you engage in your breathing patterns of inhaling and exhaling as you perform whatever exercise of your choice: walking, jogging, swimming, yoga, dancing, etc. You can use your own simple formula of breathing. Release any rigid thinking you might have and have your mind move along with your body, becoming more flexible. Keep following your breathing patterns. This saying could be: "I won't move my body with tension or fear; I will move my body with peace and grace." Or just repeat any word or words that represent how you want to show up for yourself during your exercise time. This could be as simple as "I am strong."

**Day Six:** Invite a friend or lover or family member to join you during exercise. Keep your conversation centered on things you feel grateful for in your relationship. You could exchange sentiments or memories as you move your bodies. Reminiscing, reflect on how you've loved each other's minds, hearts, souls, and bodies. Stay connected as you keep moving.

**Day Seven:** Stare into a mirror, breathe, and begin to praise your body for all it's given you. Breath, life, babies, gold medals, ability to work and earn a living, whatever it may be. Play a song that makes you feel strong, beautiful, and know that you have a body worth loving and a voice worth hearing. Lift yourself up with the lyrics.

You have now completed Week 3 *and* the first part of the book. Hopefully your heart, body, and mind are thanking you not only for the attention you've given them in the last few weeks but for not confusing one for the other. It's important to continue tending to the mind/heart/body trifecta as we dive into the next chapter and beyond. I wholeheartedly believe in this six-week process but no part of it ever ends and will hopefully only continue to evolve. So, now that you have cleared your slate, so to speak, what should you fill it with? That is what Part 2 is all about...and frankly where I think the fun begins. Shall we?

# Part Two

# Week 4

Play

> "The opposite of play is not work.
> It's depression."
>
> **—Brian Sutton-Smith**

## PLAY LIKE YOUR LIFE DEPENDS ON IT (BECAUSE IT DOES)

What this world needs more than anything is to be allowed to play! Not "play" as in go to Vegas, get drunk and forget your cares (though you're allowed that once in a while), but really play the way you did as a toddler and as a small child before all the "should dos" took over.

Our souls need to play in order to come alive and thrive. Without it, we're just going through the motions—not truly living.

We spent the first three weeks—the first part of this book—clearing your runway, so to speak; while you acknowledged and nurtured your heart, body, and mind, you also created space for your soul to land and take the lead. The best way I know to set your soul free is to play. Play is also one of the best ways to retrain your brain. We'll spend a good portion of this week exploring the connection between play and neuroscience. There have been numerous studies over the years showing the importance of play in early childhood brain development and ability to learn, but more recently there have been new studies that show the importance of play in adults.

Stuart Brown, M.D., the founder of the National Institute for Play, likes to say that "Play is a state of mind, rather than an activity."[60] What your soul needs more than anything is permission to be present, to be seen and trusted, and to sparkle as brightly as possible. The easiest way to do this is to allow your soul to play. And how do you know your soul is at play? It's the feeling you may have had while walking, jogging, swimming, dancing, or playing with your children. Many musicians and artists call it "being in the zone" or a "flow state."

> "Almost all creativity involves purposeful play."
>
> **—Abraham Maslow**

---

60   Stuart Brown, M.D., with Christopher Vaughan, *Play: How it Shapes the Brain, Opens the Imagination, and Invigorates the Soul*, (New Jersey: Avery, 2010), page 60, https://blogs.adelaide.edu.au/maths-learning/2017/06/06/book-reading-play-brain-imagination-soul/.

Psychologist Mihaly Csikszentmihalyi, who coined the term "flow state" in 1975, defines it as a state of heightened focus and blissful immersion, and it's intrinsically rewarding. In his TED Talk, "Flow: The Secret to Happiness," he describes the experience like this: "There's this focus that, once it becomes intense, leads to a sense of ecstasy, a sense of clarity: you know exactly what you want to do from one moment to the other.... Sense of time disappears. You forget yourself. You feel part of something larger."[61]

So, let's play.

## WHAT IS PLAY?

> "In every real man a child is hidden that wants to play."
>
> **—Friedrich Nietzsche**

According to play researcher Peter Gray, "From a biological evolutionary perspective, play is nature's means of ensuring that young mammals, including young human beings, acquire the skills that they need to acquire to develop successfully into adulthood."[62] And as we'll discuss more later in this chapter, play is also essential for adult growth and well-being.

---

61    Mihaly Csikszentmihalyi, "Flow, the Secret to Happiness," filmed February 2008 in Monterey, California, TED video, 18:55, https://www.ted.com/talks/mihaly_csikszentmihalyi_flow_the_secret_to_happiness.

62    Peter Gray, "The Decline of Play and Rise of Mental Disorders," filmed May 10, 2014 in Monmouth County, New Jersey, TED Navesink video, 16:03, https://www.youtube.com/watch?v=BgGEzM7iTk.

Many, many types of activities can be considered play. Gray again: "Play is not neatly defined in terms of any single characteristic; instead, it involves a constellation of characteristics, which have to do with the motives or mental framework underlying the observed behavior."[63] Scott G. Eberle, editor of the *American Journal of Play*, agrees: "Defining play is difficult because it's a moving target.... [It's] a process, not a thing."[64] Dr. Brown offers this tantalizing partial list to whet the appetite: "art, books, movies, music, comedy, flirting and daydreaming."[65] I'd add dancing and bad karaoke to that list, and my kids would insist on mentioning swimming and soccer!

Thankfully the researchers have done the work for us, and Gray has identified the top five characteristics of play that most play scholars (did you know "play scholar" could be a career choice?) can agree on. Play is 1. Self-chosen and self-directed; 2. Intrinsically motivated; 3. Guided by mental rules that leave room for creativity; 4. Imaginative; and 5. Conducted in an alert and active but relatively non-stressed frame of mind.[66] So if I'm playing a game of checkers with my kid, but they're telling me which pieces to move and I'm thinking about how quickly I can get back to work and I'm stressing out about my upcoming deadline and what to make for dinner, I'm not actually playing. But if I'm immersed in a work project that I chose for myself,

---

63   Peter Gray (2013) Definitions of Play. Scholarpedia, 8(7):30578, https://eric.ed.gov/?id=EJ1023799.

64   Ibid.

65   Saya Des Marais, MSW, "The Importance of Play for Adults," Psych-Central, updated November 9, 2022, https://psychcentral.com/blog/the-importance-of-play-for-adults#1.

66   Ibid.

exploring ideas in a flow state, and whistling, I could easily call that play.

Designer Tim Brown, the CEO of design firm IDEO, notes that "Play is not anarchy. Play has rules, especially when it's group play. When kids play tea party, or they play cops and robbers, they're following a script that they've agreed to. And it's this code negotiation that leads to productive play."[67]

Of course, we humans often like to pretend that we're doing something other than what we are, so how can you tell from the outside whether someone is actually playing or not? In Dr. Brown's book *Play*, he says to look for these qualities:

- Play is **apparently purposeless:** that is, it seems to be done for its own sake and not because it has practical value.

- Play is **voluntary:** it's not required by duty or forced upon you.

- Play has **inherent attraction:** it makes you feel good, so you want to do it.

- Play has **improvisational potential:** there is scope to put things together in new ways, to do things differently and try things out.

- People who play experience **freedom from time:** they lose a sense of time passing.

---

67   Tim Brown, "Tales of Creativity and Play," filmed May 2008 in Pasadena, California, TED video, 27:38, https://www.ted.com/talks/tim_brown_tales_of_creativity_and_play/transcript.

- People who play experience **diminished consciousness of self:** they stop thinking about their thoughts or how they look to others or whether they're making mistakes.

- People who play have **continuation desire:** they want to keep going and find ways to make it keep going.[68]

Think back over the past twenty-four hours—can you recall a moment or three when you were playing? When you saw someone else at play?

## ADULTS CAN PLAY TOO

"We don't stop playing because we grow old; we grow old because we stop playing."

**—George Bernard Shaw**

In a 2008 talk chosen as a TED "Best of the Web" pick, Dr. Brown talks about an experiment with rats who aren't allowed to play. Typically, if you take an object that is saturated in cat odor and bring it near a rat, the rat will flee and hide. It's hardwired into them, so they don't get killed by cats. And that's what happened with these rats. But the interesting thing is what happens next. There's a control

---

68   Stuart Brown, M.D., with Christopher Vaughan, *Play: How it Shapes the Brain, Opens the Imagination, and Invigorates the Soul*, (New Jersey: Avery, 2010), page 17, https://blogs.adelaide.edu.au/maths-learning/2017/06/06/book-reading-play-brain-imagination-soul/.

group in this experiment—rats who *have* been allowed to play. Those playful rats, after a while, they got curious. So, they started to explore their environment again, slowly, and try things out. And they figured out it was safe. But the rats who hadn't been allowed to play—they didn't explore. They didn't come out of hiding. They just stayed put. Until they died.[69]

Without play, they died. (Wow, that got dark fast.)

It's a sad story. But I agree with Dr. Brown that it shows the importance of play to our survival, and not just as children. When life sends a hard punch our way—a layoff, a breakup, a natural disaster—the creativity and curiosity that play brings out in us can mean both literal and emotional survival. It can mean a new way to put food on the table, pathways to fresh relationships, creative solutions to staying warm or cool or dry.

On a lighter note, play can also help us access joy. For whatever reason, I have always been drawn to playing pool. I'm not sure what it is, but it relaxes me instantly. I also like the fact that most people wouldn't consider me a pool player. When I'm playing pool, I am playful, social, goofy, and giddy. I'll act like a pool shark, dance around, jest, flirt, joke around. One of my favorite things to do is to go to a pool hall in the afternoon and hang out with a friend or my wife or a small group of friends. We talk, we laugh, we play. This kind of joyful play can make our work and our relationships better. It can lower our stress and improve our brain function well into our twilight years.

---

69  Stuart Brown, M.D., "Play Is More Than Just Fun," filmed May 2008 in Pasadena, California, TED video, 26:21, https://www.ted.com/talks/ stuart_brown_play_is_more_than_just_fun?language=en.

# Eight Play Personalities

Dr. Brown has identified eight play personalities based on neuroscience and behaviors observed in animals and humans. Some of us have a strong preference for one type of play, but most of us are a mix of a few play personalities.

- **The Joker:** The Joker loves to tell jokes, act silly, impersonate others, play practical jokes, and make people laugh. I've got a little bit of the Joker in me, though I don't like practical jokes and I make sure that my joking lifts those around me rather than roasting.

- **The Explorer:** The Explorer loves to experience new things, whether they be physical (exploring new places), intellectual (discovering new ideas), or relational (meeting and playing with new people). They are forever curious and want to explore the world around them. I have a lot of Explorer in me.

- **The Artist/Creator:** The Artist/Creator loves to play by creating and making things. This could be doodling, painting, sculpting, gardening, designing, decorating, and other creative expressions. The outcome truly doesn't matter. It's your experience and joy while you are in the flow of it. I definitely have different shades of The Artist/Creator when I play.

- **The Competitor:** The Competitor loves games with rules...and loves to win. They love to compete with themselves as well as others. Competitors can also play by watching competitive sports. I wouldn't say I am very competitive...unless it comes to playing pool, pickleball, or cornhole. I believe my wife would attest to this (insert wink). I want to acknowledge that there is a fine line between play and competing because true play has no purpose but to play...so if you're keeping score, it may no longer feel like authentic play. If you can keep score but stay detached from it, then you're free to play.

- **The Kinesthete:** The Kinesthete (doesn't exactly roll off the tongue, does it?) loves to play through movement and pushing their body to see what it can do. This play personality type could include athletes, but the joy of engaging in the activity is the focus, not the competition. The Kinesthete's play might be cartwheels, cycling, running, skipping, dancing, yoga, swimming, skipping, walking, hiking, etc. Swimming, walking, and dancing bring me a great deal of joy and peace, so I definitely have some Kinesthete in me, even if I can't pronounce it!

- **The Director:** The Director plays through planning and organizing. If you're exhausted by just reading this, you are definitely not this play personality. I hesitate to list this one because I can see how some stressed-out mom could read this and say, "I plan and organize all day and there is nothing playful about that." I would completely agree. Been there! The key differentiator here is that this personality type actually enjoys the experience of planning and organizing. This could be planning a party or big dinner, or a weekend getaway, or organizing your gatherings with friends. I can play Director once in a while, but it would definitely not be my default mode of playing.

- **The Storyteller:** The Storyteller plays through imagination and storytelling. This can be in the form of spoken word, improvisational acting, poetry, writing, and any other type of narrative expression. It could also be a father who pretends that their treehouse is Tarzan's house and creates activities around and within the fantasy. As mentioned in Week 1, my go-to is Tintin. Everything in the world can be another Tintin adventure. I believe reading and watching films can also qualify as a Storyteller personality because storytellers tend to enjoy reading, listening, and watching as much as they do sharing their stories.

- **The Collector:** The Collector plays by finding and gathering objects and experiences. They experience joy in finding new pieces or old treasures. They also revel in organizing and exhibiting their collections. Collecting can be done alone or with like-minded people within groups or organizations. Think stamp or coin collectors, antiquarians, vinyl record enthusiasts, wine connoisseurs, sports memorabilia hobbyists, etc. My wife is a big wine connoisseur, and we have endless amounts of wine. I tend to be a minimalist, so the collection of anything feels more stressful than playful, but I know it is the opposite for others.

Again, one can be a combination of these play personality types or strongly resonate with just one. However you like to play, the only rule is that you do it for play's sake. If you have a purpose in mind other than the pure joy and bliss of the experience and the moment, you are not playing.

## Play and Relationships

In relationships, play offers us a way to connect, to empathize, to build trust and intimacy, to get to know someone. One of the many things that attracted me to my wife was her ability to play at an instant. She and I could be talking about something serious, and she'd say or do something funny and it would set us off on a string of goofy conversations and actions until we were satiated, and then we'd come back to the business at hand. We would do this completely spontaneously and often.

Alternately, turning away or avoiding eye contact or attempting to look busy are all non-engaging behaviors, discouraging that emotional connection. Have you ever attempted to play with someone who just doesn't want to? I attempted this multiple times with a boss whom I couldn't stand and hoped it would help me like him better or make our interactions less awkward. Not only did he not want to play, but he also resented me for allowing the staff to play. Needless to say, the culture shifted considerably after I left, as no one at the agency dared to play. That's really sad, but you should recognize that not everyone is your playmate. I explain more on that a little later in the chapter.

Play helps us learn and practice cooperation, through its give and take and shared agreements around rules. It improves our social skills as we practice verbal and non-verbal communication, teamwork, and boundaries. It gives us a chance to try out new things and improvise. It lets us practice trusting others in low-stakes situations (or sometimes higher-stake ones, if your preferred form of play is rock climbing or skydiving!).[70]

In the years following the breakup of my relationship, I took the kids to many places around the world. They'd been traveling since they were infants, so traveling came easy to them. When we travel, we truly don't have many objectives. Some make itineraries and want to see all the

---

70  Lawrence Robinson et al., "The Benefits of Play for Adults," Help-Guide, updated November 2, 2022, https://www.helpguide.org/articles/mental-health/benefits-of-play-for-adults.htm.

sites. I find that approach exhausting. Whenever traveling, I try to maintain a "beginner's mind" and stay present to what we are exploring and discovering rather than having an itinerary to check off. So, the kids and I would explore, and they knew we didn't have any particular objective. Many times, the exploration would be on bikes. And while on those bikes, we would/could be anything: soldiers, explorers, detectives, FBI, and so on. Whatever we chose dictated the adventure to be had. Much like the hurricane adventure I mentioned in Week 1. While sheltering in a tiny bathroom in the middle of the night, waiting for the storm to pass, I created story after story and game after game based on memories of my favorite childhood book series, *Tintin*. I could tell the kids were frightened. I was too, but I knew that our imaginations would outweigh the tempest roaring outside. And I was right. The kids still recount that trip, and one of the things that they remember the most was those hours full of Tintin.

Play can also help us heal emotional wounds, by offering restorative experiences and supplanting negative beliefs with positive ones.[71] Imagine reenacting a painful scene from your childhood playground, but with a bunch of caring adults playing the parts of the other kids, and reimagining the ending to be a positive one. It's nice to *think* about a better ending, but if you *play*—act it out—it can actually help rewire your brain and nervous system. (More on the neuroplasticity piece of this later in the chapter.)

Play is also a fantastic way to build communities. The nonprofit organization InterPlay is an international community of adults who get together regularly to partic-

---

71    Ibid.

ipate in improvisational play. Founders Cynthia Winton-Henry and Phil Porter began this "active, creative approach to unlocking the wisdom of the body" in 1989, and it now has thousands of people playing in small groups worldwide.[72] And each year plenty of adults sign up for the various "Improv 101" workshops offered by local improv comedy troupes and studios. Whatever your preferred flavor of play with other humans, there's probably a group gathered somewhere. And if you prefer animal companionship, there are animals, too, who would love to frolic with you.

## Play and Work

Benefits of play at work include "more productivity, higher job satisfaction, greater workplace morale, and a decrease in employees skipping work and staff turnover."[73] What's not to love? I'd also add this: it's fun!

In the mid-2000's, I was a showrunner for the Discovery and Scripps networks and produced a few series of which I am very proud. For each series, I hand-picked my team. Everyone was a hard worker who didn't waste our time with drama. It was important for me that everyone felt they were a valued member of the team and felt appreciated. We had a lot of fun most days, but some days would become really stressful. I had the production assistant buy a disco ball, and if I felt the tension

---

72   "What is InterPlay?," InterPlay, accessed November 18, 2022, https://interplay.org/index.cfm/go/about:home/ and "Q & A: InterPlay Facts," InterPlay, accessed November 18, 2022, https://interplay.org/pdfs/InterPlayFacts.pdf.

73   Lawrence Robinson et al., "The Benefits of Play for Adults," HelpGuide, updated November 2, 2022, https://www.helpguide.org/articles/mental-health/benefits-of-play-for-adults.htm.

and stress was too high in the office, I would—without notice—turn off the lights, turn on the disco ball, and start playing disco songs. Everyone would have to drop whatever they were doing and dance their butts off until I felt the energy shift and everyone was laughing and giggling. Soon the light would be turned on, the disco ball would stop, and we'd be back at our desks, but the shift in energy was permeating, and you could see people still smiling or giggling.

Play can help you turn off the inner critic and bring in the idea generator, which helps with problem solving and creative work. It recharges you. Icebreaker games give you new ways to connect with colleagues. Crossword puzzles and board games improve brain function and memory. The release of endorphins from having fun can relieve stress and improve well-being. And the benefits last. That game of office golf where you had to putt a rubber-band ball into a company-branded coffee cup to win a stack of colored Post-it® notes doesn't just bring pleasure that afternoon. You remember it again—and your brain and body reap the benefits—every time you use those Post-it® notes or see the plastic golf club hanging in your colleague's cube or catch the eye of one of your companions as the boss takes a sip of coffee.

Some people would argue that work is "soul destroying" when you can't play, and I agree with this. I have often incorporated play into my work to boost my creativity and productivity, and if nothing else, make others around me laugh.

One time I was shooting a video segment with the amazing New York firefighters on Randall Island. It was a very hot August and the shot required multiple takes of firefighters going through a building on fire to perform a set of activities. I felt horrible sending them into the burning building in their heavy suits in ninety-eight-degree weather and high humidity, but I knew if I didn't, I wouldn't get the shots we needed. They were all amazing sports, though I did encounter an eye roll or two when I would say, "One more take!" When we stopped shooting, the firefighters decided to give me a taste of what I had put them through. They put me in one of their suits, which was way too big for me, and sent me into the burning building while my crew shot me. Not only was it pitch black and smokey in there, but I also had no idea what I should do or where I should go. So, I started doing an interpretive dance of sorts, which made no sense, but I knew it would make them chuckle. So, I was in a burning building wearing a fire uniform that I could barely move in, doing my best interpretation of Isadora Duncan. It was my way of thanking the firefighters and showing solidarity. I was later told that they would watch that video and laugh.

## Play and Creativity

> "[Play] allows the exploration of the possible."
>
> **—Stuart Brown, M.D.**

Artists of all stripes talk about play as part of their creative process, but all of us can benefit from access to creativity—and play is a wonderful avenue to get there. Let's try an experiment. Get a piece of paper and a pen and, for the next sixty seconds, sketch out your dream house. It doesn't matter how well you can draw. Just draw whatever comes to mind for the next sixty seconds. Now put your pen and paper down and start bouncing, shaking, and waving your arms and legs around like you are popcorn—pop, pop, pop around the room like nobody's business. If you can laugh or shout or yodel, go for it. Do this intensely and intentionally for sixty seconds. Then pick up your pen and paper and draw your dream house again on another piece of paper without referencing the first one. Get as creative as you'd like. There are no rules to this dream house. Sketch as freely as you can for sixty seconds and stop. Now compare the two. Are they similar or wildly different? Most people will find that their first drawings are much more conventional whereas their second ones may resemble Mickey Mouse's playhouse or the Taj Mahal.

How did you *feel* during each step? Is this something you could imagine incorporating into your life when you are trying to figure out what to do next about something?

Sometimes it helps to hear examples of other people's creative play. One of my favorites is acting improv. For a few years, I joined an ACT (American Conservatory Theater) improv group, and those nights were all about play. We were there for no other reason than to play. These weren't the usual ACT classes that professional actors attend—though some professional actors did attend, for fun and play. Each night, we would go on new adventures. I would be a cat, then a grandmother, then a tree, a queen, and so on. Some nights, we would only be assigned one role, and other nights it could be a dozen. We just played with whatever we were given and had such a blast. Every time I would leave those sessions, I felt so full of energy and genuinely happy.

I would also roleplay with my kids when they were younger. We would be detectives trying to solve a mystery or archeologists trying to find the missing treasure. At night we would be astronauts trying to find a new planet to live on and so on. Some adults take this even further with cosplay, dressing up as fictional characters,[74] often at events like the San Francisco Comic Con. Other kinds of adult group play that have been catching on in recent years are escape rooms—which combine puzzles and stories as players try to literally escape from a locked room in a finite period of time—and megagames—which "combine the physical mechanics of board games with the fluid emergent gameplay of role-playing games at large player counts (40–80 players)."[75] My wife and I sometimes do quick role reversals, which are not only funny (watching someone attempting to be you) but can also build empathy and insight for the other.

Here are some other ideas for creative play: build a sandcastle, run around like a butterfly in the garden, count the stars at night, look at the clouds and try to find an angel or a heart, build a snowman, do a bubble-blowing competition, fly a kite, jump in a mud puddle. Look at every object you interact with as if you were three years old and seeing it for the first time, wondering how you could play with it. Try face painting. Collage, color, paint, get crafty.

---

74    Alison Lurie, "5 Blockbuster Mental Health Benefits of Cosplay Costumes Online," BiNews, November 24, 2020, https://binews. org/5-blockbuster-mental-health-benefits-of-cosplay-costumes-on-line/#:~:text=They%20can%20provide%20various%20mental,dress-ing%20up%20as%20someone%20else.
75    Megagame Coalition, accessed November 19, 2022, https://megag-amecoalition.com/about/.

Make a list of the childlike activities that always make *you* feel good. Then schedule a few each week. Invite your friends over for a game night or take your partner out to throw a frisbee on the beach, go to an amusement park, or sing karaoke.

> "Play is the highest form of research."
>
> **—Albert Einstein**

## THE ROLE OF PLAY IN NEUROSCIENCE AND NEUROPLASTICITY

If you think the concept of play, and especially adult play, is a modern phenomenon, think again! Play is as old as human history. In fact, Peter Gray theorizes that play was the foundation for hunter-gatherers' social existence and key to their survival.[76] Dr. Brown notes that "divinely superfluous neurons existed many, many moons ago and enabled art and play to take place. Play has been part of human life for a very long time. And it's hardwired into us. (In yet another rat experiment, rats without a cerebral cortex were still able to play—the ability to play was tied to the survival parts of the brain.[77] I'd be willing to bet that's true for humans, too, though I'd rather not experiment to find out!)

76   Peter Gray, "Play as a Foundation for Hunter-Gatherer Social Existence," *American Journal of Play*, Volume 1, Article 4 (Spring 2009), Museum of Play, https://www.journalofplay.org/sites/www.journalofplay.org/files/pdf-articles/1-4-article-hunter-gatherer-social-existence.pdf.

77   The Aspen Institute, "The Neuroscience of Play," YouTube, https://www.youtube.com/watch?v=hrw68eID4Zk.

Dr. Allan Schore's early research on attunement between babies and mothers began to connect the biology and psychology of the infant mind,[78] and more recent scientific research using brain scans is further proving that research and adding more insight. In the Princeton Baby Lab, a group of scientists and psychologists (Elise Piazza, Liat Hasenfratz, Uri Hasson, and Casey Lew-Williams) developed a dual-brain neuroimaging system to measure what happened when an adult interacted naturally with a baby or toddler. They found unexpected "coupling" between the baby and adult brains as they interacted. According to Piazza, "The adult and child seem to form a feedback loop.... The adult's brain seemed to predict when the infants would smile, the infants' brains anticipated when the adult would use more 'baby talk,' and both brains tracked joint eye contact and joint attention to toys. So, when a baby and adult play together, their brains influence each other in dynamic ways."[79]

This is good news when adult and baby are in sync, but can lead to attachment issues and other developmental trauma when the connection breaks down (like with autism or a mentally unhealthy, abusive, or absent caregiver). But the more we learn, the more we understand how neuroplasticity may be used later in life—often via play—for healing and reparenting. All those new age encounter groups in the 1970s about the inner child and rebirthing actually have science to back them up!

---

78    Kathy Brous, "Allan Schore: What is the Self?," WordPress, Posted May 16, 2014, https://attachmentdisorderhealing.com/allan-schore/.

79    Liz Fuller-Wright, ""Baby and Adult Brains 'sync up' During Play," ScienceDaily, January 9, 2020, https://www.sciencedaily.com/releases/2020/01/200109163956.htm.

Neuroscience research shows the potential for play therapy can be used to create new neural pathways.[80] Kathy Brous, author of *Don't Try This Alone: The Silent Epidemic of Attachment Disorder*, summarizes the immense impact of this new science on humans with developmental trauma (emphasis mine):

> If we can sit for an hour and attune to another human willing to share our emotional state and help us learn to gradually shift and modulate it, we learn to "regulate." Brain scans now show that **we can literally repair the neural circuits** which remained painfully out of tune when we didn't receive human attunement as kids.[81]

My point is that playing can literally change your mind. They say insanity is doing the same things over and over again expecting different results. Therefore, if you want your life to be different, you have to live it differently. In order to do something differently, you have to think differently, and the easiest and most enjoyable way to change your mind is to play.

---

80   Anne Stewart et al., "Neuroscience and the Magic of Play Therapy," *International Journal of Play Therapy*, 25, no.1 (January 2016):4-13, https://doi.org/10.1037/pla0000016.

81   Kathy Brous, "Allan Schore: What is the Self?," WordPress, Posted May 16, 2014, https://attachmentdisorderhealing.com/allan-schore/.

# Neurons That Fire Together Wire Together

The founder of the Arrowsmith School, Barbara Arrowsmith-Young, was once labeled as "retarded" by her school teachers when they observed her struggling to learn how to read and write in elementary school. Later, she learned she had severe dyslexia. During graduate school, Barbara set out to build herself a better brain by using the principles of neuroplasticity. Neuroplasticity is the theory that the nerve cells in our brains and nervous systems are malleable, and that the brain changes its structure with each different activity it performs. Devising a simple game using flash cards and repetition, Barbara successfully rewired her brain to perform simple tasks such as reading a clock, which she was previously unable to do. At the end of several weeks, not only could she read clocks faster than the average person, but she also started to understand what people were saying as they said it (another impossible task). She has now dedicated her life to sharing her tools for success with others.

Nothing in the brain changes without neurons changing. Neuroplasticity is the capacity of the nervous system to make new neural connections.[82] The brain contains roughly 100 billion neurons, each of which "is capable of making thousands, sometimes hundreds of thousands, connections with other neurons using chemicals called neurotransmitters that transmit electrical signals along complex cellular pathways."[83] These path-

---

82    "Neuroplasticity," Dictionary.com, accessed November 20, 2022, https://www.dictionary.com/browse/neuroplasticity.
83    Paul Tingen, "Using Mindfulness to Rewire the Brain," Tingen, 2012, http://tingen.org/mindfulness-rewire-brain/.

ways, called neural pathways, become more dug in with reuse, much like the paths of cows through fields became packed-down footpaths and then dirt roads and eventually the streets of Boston, "propelling us to keep repeating similar feelings, thoughts and actions. Every time we fire off a particular pathway, it increases the likelihood of us doing it again."[84] Yet play naturally redirects neurons, and once you're able to make that shift and free your neurons, so to speak, you can learn new ways of being and build new habits.

So, in short, play can rewire your brain. When we start playing, we're allowing our neurons to redirect. That redirection gives us the ability to recreate over and over again. The act of play offers us new possibilities that would not be present without it. And the more we play, the more the neurons are allowed to play, explore, and redirect. And if we want to channel that toward becoming a greater parent or a better artist or more present partner, we can. The possibilities are truly endless.

## FIND YOUR PLAYMATES

"Life must be lived as play."

**—Plato**

How often you play and with whom you play is completely up to you, but I would highly suggest that you make time to do so. And the people you pick to play with need to

---

84    Ibid.

know that the main purpose of your activity is to play—so any other objectives (such as getting a workout or taking time away from your kids) are secondary.

I really think that one of the factors in me becoming a slow-boiling frog during my so-called "Walking Dead" years before my breakup was because I had stopped playing, entirely. When the kids were babies and toddlers, I spent much of those early years on my own because my partner was traveling most of the time. To make matters worse, we had bought a gorgeous Tuscan villa in Sonoma, CA, which was stunning but a completely impractical place to live. My partner was gone most of the time, and I was out there on a mountain, which felt like the middle of nowhere, with two toddlers and a puppy. I could have screamed at the top of my lungs, and no one would have heard me. It took twenty minutes just to get to the nearest store, forty minutes to the nearest hospital. Friends and family would visit from time to time and comment on how gorgeous and serene it all was, and I felt like I was slowly going mad. Have you ever watched *The Shining*? "All work and no play makes Shirin a dull girl." Hours, days, and weeks blended together into one sleepless, restless blur. When my partner was home, I was cranky and irritable. We eventually moved to Marin and life became saner, but the deadness really didn't leave me until I was jolted awake when we broke up. As you can imagine, the last thing someone who is as broken as I was at the time wants to do is to play—but I truly believe it was one of the major factors missing from my life.

In the early days of the breakup, friends and family would come by. They would bring food and shower me with kindness and warmth. They became my lifeline. Some friends who I thought would be there didn't show up, at least in the way I believed they would. But other friends who I didn't expect to be there for me showed up out of the blue. One such friend is someone I had not seen for years. I have a great deal of fun with many of my friends, but she and I play every time we're together. We're just goofy together. We say silly things, we do silly things, and our activities have no other objective than playing. We've been to parties together where we've danced our butts off. We've gotten lost and made an adventure out of it. We've roamed endlessly, skipped down trails, engaged in much mischief, and continue frolicking at a moment's notice.

A spiritual teacher of mine would say to be aware of who in your life expands or contracts your heart. Michelle, my playmate, expanded my heart when I needed it most. I think she did so partially because I was hurting, but I believe a part of her also knew that I would play along. From the first time we reconnected, she made me chuckle. My waters can run quite deep and, in those days, quite dark, but she was an instant light, and I couldn't get enough. I had and still have other friends who I dive deep with, but I didn't want to with Michelle nor did I feel I had to. More than anything, it was the frequency and the repetition of our gaiety (pun intended) that became a healing force.

I think people can sense their playmates in much the same way they can tell that someone could become a good friend or a lover. When you know, you know. I don't play with all my friends. Or more accurately, I do not play the same with all my friends. The same way we don't go to a romcom movie expecting a thriller, not all friends are there for the same experience. I have two best friends. One is brilliant and very heady. We share the same heritage and culture, so she feels like a sister to me, and we often have philosophical discussions. My other BFF is my spiritual sister, who I've known for more than twenty years. We both started our journey around the same time and can go very, very, very deep—instantly. I have a handful of other close friends, and my own sister is also very near and dear to me, but I don't play the same way or to the same extent with all of them. They all expand my heart and are my tribe, but are not necessarily playmates all the time.

At the time of this writing, I have been with my wife for more than two years, and she and I also play. It has become an integral part of our relationship. So just as easily as we communicate, partner in different activities together, parent the kids, work, take care of our home, and so on, we also play. Our play feels rich, silly, and intimate, but always without purpose or an expectation of an outcome. It is play for play's sake—which is the only way play should be played.

Two of my favorite playmates are my kids, who are currently thirteen and fifteen. They remind me every day to play. Somedays I am much better at it than other days. My wife, the kids, and I can be super goofy and frolic a great deal. The other day we almost got into some trouble because we were playing a game of who could jump a fence the best without realizing we were trespassing at a water treatment plant!

# Week 4

## The Daily Purge

How is your Daily Purge going? It's Week 4...have you landed on a practice that you'd like to continue through Week 6 (or even the rest of your life)? Do you want to try a different way of purging for the coming week? As a reminder, some options you can choose from are writing, doodling, singing, dancing, jogging, and walking. I've even known people who found cycling or yoga to be a great purge activity! Are you purging at the same time every day? Is that time working well for you? Again, it's okay to make adjustments if it's not. The Daily Purge is there to support *you*, and not the other way around.

# Week 4

## Exercise: Learning to Play Again

**Day One:** Think of a simple physical play activity you used to love as a kid, such as bouncing a ball, playing with a yo-yo, or skateboarding. Spend ten minutes doing that activity. How do you feel? What do you want to do next?

**Day Two:** Put on your favorite dance song(s) and boogie for ten minutes like no one is watching. It doesn't matter if you think you can't dance. You can! After ten minutes, take a moment to notice how you feel—or just keep dancing if you'd like.

**Day Three:** Karaoke time—let's hear ten minutes of karaoke to your favorite song(s). (You can find karaoke versions of many songs with a web or YouTube search. Or just sing along with the original artist.) It doesn't matter if you think you can't sing. You can!

**Day Four:** Find the nearest playground and swing for ten minutes. Bonus points if you sing or whistle while doing so. If there's not a swing nearby that works for your body type, spend ten minutes making silly faces with a child or an animal.

**Day Five:** Time to break out your crayons, colored pencils, or markers and a piece of paper. A plain sheet of printer paper or a blank page of your journal will do, but you're welcome to use something larger—a posterboard, the backside of some wrapping paper, a side of that cardboard box you've been meaning to recycle. Get comfortable, and let yourself imagine paradise. Now draw an image of what you believe is paradise...but do so with the opposite hand than the one you write with. If you're ambidextrous, try this exercise with your eyes closed. When you're done drawing, take a moment to notice how you feel—and what you like about your drawing.

**Day Six:** Who is your favorite movie character of all time? What does that character look like? How do they sound? How do they dress? How do they move? Dress up as your favorite movie character (to the best of your ability) and become that character—same accent, same walk, same gestures, and so on. If you're feeling shy, you can do this in the privacy of your own home (but make sure to peek at yourself in the mirror!). If you're feeling brave, head outside for a walk around the neighborhood or take a video and share it with a friend.

**Day Seven:** Play role reversal with a friend, family member, or spouse. (For best results, pick someone who likes to say "yes" to new things.) Take turns showing each other what the other is like in different situations, for instance:

- when they're excited

- when they don't like something

- when they wake up

- when they go shopping

- when they drive (or when they are a passenger, if they don't have a driver's license)

- when they eat a melting popsicle or ice cream cone

When you're finished playing, take a moment to each share your favorite of the other's impressions.

\* \* \*

We've come to the end of Week 4, but hopefully it is just the beginning of your play journey. I simply love to play... so much so that I've researched the idea of creating adult play centers. It wouldn't be a gym, or community center, spa, or spiritual center, but would have elements of all. A place where adults could go at any time to pause, purge, and play—simply because. There truly is no greater gift you can give your soul than to allow it play—and please don't stop. Ever.

# Week 5
## Find Your True North

### FINDING YOUR SOUL IN A SOUL-DEPRIVED WORLD

As of the writing of this book, there are more than 8 million mobile apps in the world,[85] nearly 2 billion websites,[86] and more than 30,000 TV channels.[87] Computers that would have taken up an entire building in the past can now be worn on our wrists. We're able to view a human-made robot "roam" around Mars and can see images of Icarus, a star nine billion light years away. Yet we seem to grapple with some of the most basic aspects of being human and

---

85    John Koetsier, "There Are Now 8.9 Million Mobile Apps, and China Is 40% of Mobile App Spending," *Forbes*, accessed November 21, 2022, https://www.forbes.com/sites/johnkoetsier/2020/02/28/there-are-now-89-million-mobile-apps-and-china-is-40-of-mobile-app-spending/?sh=6049738921dd.

86    "Total Number of websites," Internet Live Stats, accessed November 22, 2022, https://www.internetlivestats.com/total-number-of-websites/.

87    30,000+ Live TV Channels – No Additional Costs," GOWORLDTV, accessed November 22, 2022, https://goworldtv.com/channel-listing.

how to live harmoniously with other humans on the only known inhabitable planet. Why is that? Why is it that in school, they teach you math, science, history, English, and sometimes physical education, but little about mental, emotional, and spiritual health?

It's not surprising that our world is in constant turmoil and has what I call a low collective Emotional Intelligence. There's so much emphasis in education on transmitting knowledge for the attainment of a great job, which is tied to status and money, which is attached to the purchasing of things, which all culminates in a lot of ego and materialism. Yet a recent survey showed that "higher levels of spirituality are strongly correlated with higher life satisfaction."[88] What would it be like if, from the beginning, we were taught self-awareness—if not spirituality or soulfulness—at an early age?

Many people tend to think of soul seeking as this wavy gravy new age thing that one does by going to yoga or a weekend retreat. They equate it with meditation or joining an ashram in India. Although it can be included in those activities, I believe soul seeking is one of the most difficult, humbling, courageous, and deeply honest choices one can make. And to commit to it regardless of what one hits up against (and you are guaranteed to hit up against a lot) is, in my opinion, one of life's greatest challenges and accomplishments. There's also this notion that spirituality is always peaceful, calm, and serene. While it can definitely be all of these, it is often dark, scary, uncomfortable...and well, not so pretty. So, if you have an image

---

88   "New Survey: One in Five Americans are Spiritual but Not Religious," PRRI, November 6, 2017, https://www.prri.org/press-release/new-survey-one-five-americans-spiritual-not-religious/.

in your mind of what your journey will look like, please do yourself a favor and erase it—now! It will most likely look nothing like what you have in mind and having an image may only lead to self-criticism, which can hinder you from being exactly who and where you are. There is no set way to be. Truly come as you are and allow everything to unfold as it should. The Buddhists say, "Don't push the river." You don't need to control anything. Just learn to swim and dance with the all there is. And no matter what, don't quit.

This is, frankly, how Siddhartha Gautama became the Buddha. He didn't reach enlightenment by accident or by studying or working hard (although studying and exploring were certainly part of his path). He was born into a life of leisure and left that life to find the meaning of life, which ended up becoming what we know as Buddhism, and he did so—sitting under the Bodhi tree—by facing his demons. He faced all of his demons head on until he reached the other side, and then decided to teach others what he learned.

Spirituality isn't this lofty thing that only privileged white people do on their off time when they go to yoga. Finding your soul is a matter of diving in deep and soul-excavating, looking in every nook and cranny and being with what is, not pushing anything under the carpet. That's how Siddhartha Gautama found enlightenment. And that's the path for us as well.

In order to live a fulfilling and rich life, we must find or reclaim our sense of connectedness and our place in the universe. It doesn't matter what your religion is...or even if you have one. You can be an atheist and still believe there is a universal energy that connects us. Even if you don't believe in a universal force, I ask for the purpose of this process that you trust there is something greater at work and that it is there for you to reclaim and align with.

> "Once you believe in yourself and see your soul as divine and precious, you'll automatically be converted to a being who can create miracles."
>
> **—Wayne Dyer**

Spirituality isn't a thing that one does in their spare time. It really does compound. The Buddhists talk about the Lotus, the idea that the more you open up, the more you open up. It's not a journey where you start somewhere, you end somewhere, and that's it. This book is meant to (hopefully) shift something within you, so that you live from the inside out and feel connected to the greater universe. So that everything you do is contained in that.

I'm very much *not* trying to say, "Hey, drop your life as an electrical engineer and go join an ashram because that's the way of the universe." Be that electrical engineer. Or a poet or a postal worker or an account executive. Do exactly what you do. But do it from a soulful place and for the greater good of humanity and the universe. Living a soulful life in this world is only truly worthwhile if you are making your life and the lives of those you touch more meaningful and profound and better. If we all do that, hopefully we will find ourselves in a much different, better world.

"The only journey is the journey within."

**—Rainer Maria Rilke**

# SPIRITUALITY IS NOT A RELIGION

"Spirituality is not religion. It is a path for us to generate happiness, understanding, and love, so we can live deeply each moment of our life."

**—Thich Nhat Hanh**

The definition of religion is "the belief in and worship of a superhuman controlling power, especially a personal God or gods."[89] The definition of spirituality is "the quality of being concerned with the human spirit or soul as opposed to material or physical things."[90] Two very different beliefs that can coexist and do not negate one another. Why is this important? Because I often hear people say, "I am Christian and therefore spiritual already" or, alternatively, "I am Catholic and therefore can't ascribe to spirituality as they are in conflict." In fact, you can be religious but not spiritual, like one in

89  Dictionary.com, accessed November 22, 2022, https://www.lexico.com/definition/religion.
90  Dictionary.com, accessed November 22, 2022, https://www.lexico.com/definition/spirituality.

five Americans—according to a 2017 survey by PRRI, the Public Religion Research Institute—or spiritual but not religious, like another one in five, or both or neither (evenly split between the remaining Americans).[91]

There is an amazing energy to collectively being in a soulful space with others, and that can be found through both spirituality and organized religion. I like to attend spiritual gatherings at Spirit Rock myself. But spirituality is freeform, which is different from an organized religion that has a specific doctrine that you have to follow. Organized religion has a lot of dos and don'ts. With spirituality, if it's done as it's meant to be, you pick and choose what works for you. You can be spiritual while you're doing the dishes. It's a very personal and freeform way of discovering oneself. Spirituality is self-designed from the inside out.

Interestingly, scientists have recently discovered the "neurobiological home"[92] of spirituality. Neuroscience researchers at Columbia University and Yale University discovered that the parietal cortex of the brain lit up on an fMRI scan when subjects entered a transcendent state generated by their own personally meaningful spiritual experiences, whether that transcendence "involve[d] communion with God, nature, or humanity."[93] It turns

91 "New Survey: One in Five Americans are Spiritual but Not Religious," PRRI, November 6, 2017, https://www.prri.org/press-release/new-survey-one-five-americans-spiritual-not-religious/.

92 Bill Hathaway, "Where the Brain Processes Spiritual Experiences," Yale University, May 29, 2018, https://news.yale.edu/2018/05/29/where-brain-processes-spiritual-experiences.

93 Ephrat Livni, "Columbia and Yale scientists found the spiritual part of our brains—religion not required," Quartz, May 30, 2018, https://qz.com/1292368/columbia-and-yale-scientists-just-found-the-spiritual-part-of-our-brains/.

out that biologically it's about connecting with something greater than yourself, whatever that may be. Our ancestors may have turned most often to religion to get there, and you certainly can take that pathway, but science confirms that you don't have to.

## SPIRITUALITY VS. SPIRITUAL BYPASS

You may have heard the phrase "spiritual bypassing." At its core, spiritual bypassing is a way of hiding behind spirituality to avoid the hard stuff. The term was first used by psychotherapist John Welwood in the 1980s. As Welwood later explained in an interview, "Spiritual bypassing is a term I coined to describe a process I saw happening in the Buddhist community I was in, and also in myself. Although most of us were sincerely trying to work on ourselves, I *noticed a widespread tendency to use spiritual ideas and practices to sidestep or avoid facing unresolved emotional issues, psychological wounds, and unfinished developmental tasks.* When we are spiritually bypassing, we often use the goal of awakening or liberation to try to rise above the raw and messy side of our humanness before we have fully faced and made peace with it. We may also use our notion of absolute truth to disparage or dismiss relative human needs, feelings, psychological problems, relational difficulties, and developmental deficits."[94] (Emphasis mine.)

Spiritual bypassing can be dangerous. It can be hurtful—to ourselves and to those around us. And it also seems to be as normal a part of human existence as any

---

94    John Welwood, "Human Nature, Buddha Nature," interview by Tina Fossella, *Meditation Magazine*, Tricycle, Spring 2011, https://tricycle. org/magazine/human-nature-buddha-nature/.

other kind of avoidance behavior. As a defense mechanism, it can serve at times to protect us from something we're not yet ready to face. So, I share about it not to shame you but to make you aware, so you can work on those parts of yourself when spiritual bypassing arises... and so that you might recognize when it might be at play in those around you.

Here are some examples of spiritual bypassing:

- Spiritual window shopping. Meditating when you feel like it, going to a weekend retreat here and there, taking yoga classes, wearing Buddhist attire and jewelry, saying Namaste, and drinking pressed juices and such are all good and fine, but they don't add up to you being a spiritual or soulful person. As mentioned earlier in the book, this was my biggest spiritual bypassing. I would dabble in spirituality (what I've dubbed half-ass spirituality) whenever convenient or whenever I was somehow in trouble—bartering with G-O-D to get me out of whatever mess I was in—and as soon as I was out, I would forget my spirituality. I would also get frustrated when things weren't going my way even though I was doing all the right things: practicing "the law of attraction," meditating (when convenient), chanting "Nam-myoho-renge-kyo" so I would get something I wanted, and so on. I now joke that I always get what I want, but never on my timeline. If you're trying to control your spirituality so you have a specific outcome, you are spiritual bypassing.

- Pretending not to be angry. Suppression is a form of spiritual bypass, and it ends up showing up in other ways. People who are passive aggressive tend to be in this category, as are people who only look on the bright side. Anger is a very valid and real emotion like any other, and there are many ways of expressing and working through anger that are constructive. Suppression isn't one of them.

- Minimizing an issue or situation or brushing it under the carpet. This is also often called "gaslighting" when one person is minimizing an issue that someone else is raising—and rightly so for the amount of damage it can do to relationships—but it can be just as spiritually damaging to do it to yourself. I've been on the receiving end of gaslighting, and I can tell you that it is silent, cruel, and prolonged torture. It made me question my sanity, and I believe it is one of the cruelest things you can do to another human. People may not always agree with you, and you may not have the same perspective, but if they are sharing their experience, thoughts, and emotions with you, give them the gift of listening to them. It may not be your truth, but it is their truth and it is worth acknowledging. People want to be seen and acknowledged. Give them that gift, even if you don't agree.

- Blindly following someone as a guru, swami, sage, or master. There are many well-qualified spiritual healers in the world, but any legitimate spiritual leader will tell you that they are not your master. To follow someone blindly without question is not only spiritual bypassing but it also sets you well on the way to becoming a cult devotee. The Buddhist sage Lin-Chi once told a monk, "If you meet the Buddha on the road, kill him," meaning that those who think they've found all the answers are by far not a guru and should not be confused for one.

- Using psychedelic drugs recreationally to escape your reality and avoid commitment to your growth.[95] I say this with full acknowledgement that medical and therapeutic use of psychoactive drugs such as ayahuasca and psilocybin can provide profound insights and breakthroughs when administered under the guided and intentional care of a professional. I am referring to recreational use.

- Blaming everyone around you instead of looking at where you too may hold some responsibility.[96] One of the most liberating choices I've made in the past few years is to

---

95   Altheia, "What Is Spiritual Bypassing? (Beware of These 10 Types)" *LonerWolf*, August 28, 2022, https://lonerwolf.com/what-is-spiritual-bypassing/.
96   Ibid.

own my part in matters and offer a mea culpa as soon as I recognize my mistakes. I used to think doing so would make me look weak and it would leave me without armor. I've learned that it's incredibly powerful to own your faults and that "armor" was creating more internal harm than any apology would ever do.

- Putting all your faith in a higher power to resolve your problems.[97] There's an old joke about a man in a flood. As the waters rise, first a neighbor knocks on his front door to offer him a ride out of town, then someone else comes by with a boat, and finally as he's standing on his roof with the water up to his waist, a helicopter arrives. To each he says, "You go on, God will save me." Finally, the water rises above his head and the man drowns. When he reaches the gates of heaven, devastated, he cries out to God, "Why didn't you save me?" And God answers, "What more were you waiting for? I sent a car and a boat and a helicopter!" Sometimes we need to accept a helicopter ride, or even learn to drive.

---

97    Ibid.

So let yourself acknowledge what's difficult, recognize your own needs, and feel your feelings. For more about spiritual bypassing, I highly recommend the spring 2011 interview with John Welwood in *Meditation Magazine*, "Human Nature, Buddha Nature," which can be found online at:

If you are going to read only one resource I mention in this book, let it be this one.

## WHEN BYPASSING NO LONGER WORKS

> "Acceptance looks like a passive state, but in reality it brings something entirely new into this world. That peace, a subtle energy vibration, is consciousness."
>
> **—Eckhart Tolle**

"To forgive is to set a prisoner free and discover that the prisoner was you."

**—Lewis B. Smedes**

In order to find our True North, we must learn to accept and forgive. If you had told me this in the early days of my breakup, I would have ushered you out of my house. That was the last thing I wanted to hear. I had invested everything I had (and didn't have) into my relationship, and within twenty minutes, it was all undone. In hindsight, the devolution of our relationship started years earlier, but I (as the ever-loyal slow-boiling frog) did not see it coming.

Even many years later, I remember that night clearly. I came home from work, and it was one of the very rare evenings when she was home before me. She was watching a program with the kids. I made the kids something to eat, we played with them for a while, and put them to bed. We typically would cook dinner for ourselves and talk about our day. That night, she pulled two beers out of the fridge and said we should talk. We went into the living room, and I thought something had happened to her that she wanted to discuss. Instead, she said the words I thought would never come out of her mouth: "I think it's time we part ways."

I had supported my partner emotionally, I was the primary caretaker of the kids even though I was also an executive of a startup, I had helped her business grow, and just as she began to enjoy the gains of her success, she called it off. She quit us, selfishly! The rest of the twenty minutes was a blur of words from her that felt empty, hypocritical, and narcissistic. I remember her mentioning something about how she wanted us to remain a family and me thinking that this was like my mom saying she didn't want to be my mother anymore. It was THAT surreal to me. And worst of all, I had no Plan B. I felt raw, stupid, angry, betrayed, and frightened as I knew in my heart that the family that we had was gone, and I had no idea what it would do to the kids.

When the twenty minutes were over, I told her that she could sleep in the guestroom, that we would speak with the kids in the morning, and that she had to leave immediately after, as this was no longer her home. I didn't sleep for a second that night and it would become the first of many, many nights I lay awake, but in the middle of that first night, I took off my commitment ring and whispered, "Never again." I didn't intend the words as a proclamation, and frankly the ease of how they flowed out of me was surprising...and telling. The slow-boiling frog got the message FINALLY and jumped out. I think "never again" was half-knowing that I would never let her get anywhere close to my heart again as she could not be trusted (yes, she is currently in my Shield category and spent many years in the Taser category), but I was also clear that I would never allow myself to be in that position with anyone ever again. I had compromised and shrunk myself so much in order to receive her love because I did not believe I could be loved for exactly who I am...and in the process completely lost who I am. So, I lay there that very first night—and many, many nights after—staring at the ceiling, wondering what to do. As mentioned earlier in the book, my mantra became #betterthanthis. I knew my heart was in extreme pain, my thoughts weren't serving me, and my soul was longing for something I could not comprehend.

> "Forgiveness is a transformative act because it asks you to be a more empathetic and compassionate person, thereby making you better than the person you were when you were first hurt."
>
> **—Kamand Kojouri**

I truly thought I could never forgive my ex—how she quit me after twenty-two years of friendship and partnership and broke up our family for her own benefit...but I have—not for her—but because I knew that if I would not... could not...that I would not be able to go far in my spiritual journey. But here's the thing: forgiveness is not a one-time act. It is sometimes a very slow walk toward freedom. In the West, we often want things wrapped up neatly and quickly. How often have you heard people say, "forgive and let go," like one can just toss twenty-two years of friendship and partnership in the trash and be on with it? It doesn't work like that, at least not if you are truly seeking. For me, forgiveness has been a slow drip, but every time I feel it, it is powerful and freeing. Any person co-parenting with an ex knows the day-to-day challenges. It's like firing someone and having to continue working with them closely day in and day out. But I wouldn't be who I am today if I had not forgiven...and continue to forgive.

"Pain is inevitable. Suffering is optional."

—Haruki Murakami

Forgiveness and acceptance go hand in hand. The practice of acceptance, much like forgiveness, is a practice. The more you do it, the more you are able to do it. What is very important to understand is that acceptance is not complacency. You are not acquiescing to someone who has hurt you or something that is not okay. You are simply accepting that it has happened and not denying any part of it. It simply is what it is—good or bad. It is what you do with it that makes all the difference. I have attended Jack Kornfield's talks and meditations many times. I love hearing him speak, as he is kind, clearly woke, and funny. One of his sayings is, "Ah, this too." He says that as we meditate or experience life, we are bound to be met with thoughts, feelings, emotions, actions, and situations we do not expect or like. But instead of fighting against it, denying it, or resisting it, simply welcome it and observe it with a simple "Ah, this too," and after sitting with it for a while, let it go. That is acceptance. It's allowing things to be exactly as they are and finding your grace within it all. This doesn't mean you can't stand up for your rights or that you allow people to take advantage of you. Your work is to show up as fiercely as you feel inside but to do so with acceptance and forgiveness in your heart. I can imagine that may sound like a contradiction to some of you, but it is not. Imagine yourself as a warrior of love walking through a war. You can't deny that the war is happening. It's all around you. But your job is to not let that war define you and for you to do whatever is in your capacity to continue to emanate love, peace, and forgiveness—regardless of what comes at you. That is a true warrior.

> "The path of forgiveness is not an easy one. On this path, we must walk through the muddy shoals of hatred and anger and make our way through grief and loss to find the acceptance that is the hallmark of forgiveness."
>
> —**Desmond Tutu,** *The Book of Forgiving*

## THE TRIBE OF YOU

People often confuse the soul and spirit. I believe true spirituality is the dance between the two. Spirit is also often referred to as consciousness, awareness, higher self, infinite energy, and the "all that is." It's about inter-connectedness and oneness. And our souls are what emanate from within, distinct from our minds, bodies, and hearts. It's about the essence of a unique self. Both are vital. The way I see it, spirit is the "all that is," and our souls are our part in it. So, spirituality is our souls dancing with the spirit.

The reason we spent so much time in Part 1 detoxing the mind, body, and heart is to clear the path to finding our soul. When there is no distinction or awareness of which part of you is running the show, it's hard to know what to do. A few years into my spiritual journey, I had the privilege of attending a retreat known as the Hoffman Process. I say privilege because it is not cheap—wish it was so that more people could have access to it—and because it is a very unique opportunity to gain a great deal of self-awareness. A few of my friends had gone through the Hoffman Process and really benefited from it. It wasn't something I felt I had to do, but I knew that I would gain new insights if I did. I went in with a commitment "to live and love from a higher place," and I got that and so much more. Leaving Hoffman, I could truly say that it was the very first time in my life I felt complete without having to look to or for something outside of myself, and that feeling hasn't changed. If anything, it has become stronger. I learned tools and concepts that I continue to use in my day-to-day life. I am also absolutely convinced that I would not be with my wife had it not been for the process because I became crystal clear about who I wanted (and didn't want) as a partner. I met my partner, now wife, five months after.

The Hoffman Process describes itself as "a 7-day soul searching, healing retreat of transformation & development for people who feel stuck in one or more important areas of their life."[98] The retreat is offered many times throughout the year in both California and Connecticut and sells out well in advance. Each group is limited to forty people. In my session, there were three coaches and one trainee leading the group, and they make it very clear that there is not to be any contact with the outside world for the time you're there. I gained a great deal of awareness through the Hoffman Process, but one of the

98    "Transform Your Life," Hoffman Institute, accessed November 22, 2022, https://www.hoffmaninstitute.org/.

most profound distinctions I learned is what the Hoffman Process calls the Quadrinity: it is how your heart, mind, body, and soul work/dance together to make the you of you. But in order for our Quadrinity to connect with everything outside of ourselves, we need to tap into spirit. How? By going within and examining what is happening and then reaching out...opening up to our Higher Power/ universal energy/"the all that is" for guidance and connectedness. It is this union/dance that creates all the magic. It is how we align our inner compass with the ever-moving energy of the universe. That, I believe, is the true meaning of spirituality.

Since the retreat, I've made a habit of regularly checking in with my Quadrinity. I now call it my "inner tribe." So now when I'm up against something, I sit with it. I literally sit there and check in with my mind, body, heart, and soul to see who is at the wheel, so to speak. If I am anxious or in a panic about something, it is certainly not my soul driving the bus. The culprit is usually our minds, but sometimes the body is fatigued, or our heart has contracted. So, we have a little internal assembly of sorts where we all gather, check in, and then connect with our Higher Power. Doing this alone has done wonders. Knowing what part of you is triggered and needs tending is so very key to working through any issue.

## EVERYDAY MINDFULNESS

I hope in this chapter and book, I've been able to convey that spiritual work is not some fluffy fun thing you do when you have the time for it. In my (maybe not so humble) opinion, it is what our world is deprived of and the cause of so much angst in our world. It doesn't take much to realize that our world—with all of its riches, resources, pomp, and circumstance—is at its core dysfunctional. We're constantly making things bigger, faster, and more...and for what? We can now Google pretty much anything—information and content is at our fingertips, and we can connect to anyone in almost any part of the world and travel to it. There are constant amazing new discoveries in the worlds of science, math, technology and health...and yet, depression, suicide, mass shootings, hate, racism, and wars are at an all-time high. So, we work functionally, but are broken spiritually. Why? I believe it's because spirituality is misunderstood as some airy-fairy notion and considered secondary to everything else. So, no matter what we build, the degrees we earn, the money we make, the power we have, or what we buy, it will never fulfill our souls...at least not for very long because they are ego-based. So how do we bring our soul and spirit into our daily lives? Boldly and consistently. In one of the workshops I went to, they would repeatedly remind us that "everything is everything." That means nothing is left out. So, it matters how you treat your children when no one else is watching, how you work, what you eat, what you think, what you do, what you buy, how you walk through every day. If you are out there "saving" the world but not tending to your spouse, your children, or loved ones, you're ultimately feeding your ego rather than meeting and serving the world from your soul.

For me, everyday spirituality means trying to be as present and mindful as possible as often as I can be. My days can get very frenetic as I tend to have my fingers and toes in many places at once. I used to feel a little embarrassed by it until someone told me the correct term for it is Serial Entrepreneur. Kidding aside, being present to the moment is incredibly powerful, grounding and rewarding...but it can also be very challenging. According to physicist Max Planck, on average, we are present for ten to the negative forty-three seconds (which is much, much smaller than a single second) before we're back in thought.[99]

Buddhist monks whose main intention and goal is to stay present are said to be present for a few minutes before falling back into thought and having to re-prompt themselves into being present. So, while I believe it is good to be as present as possible, what seems to be more realistic is to be mindful and self-aware.[100]

Through my spiritual practice, I am certainly far less reactionary than I used to be. I also don't wake in the middle of the night in a panic anymore because I am clear it is only my monkey mind going wild. All I need to do is to tell it to sit in the corner and remind myself that at that moment in time, my only job is to sleep.

This also makes me more patient with my kids, which any parent of a teen can tell you is very handy, and I believe it makes me a more forgiving, giving, and loving

99  David B. Seaburn, Ph.D., L.M.F.T., "How Long Does the Present Last?," *Psychology Today*, October 11, 2016, https://www.psychologytoday.com/us/blog/going-out-not-knowing/201610/how-long-does-the-present-last.

100 Andrew Fenn, Venerable Sampasadana (a Buddhist monk), et al., "How long is 'now', the gap between the past and the future? (continued)," *New Scientist*, Issue 3324, March 6, 2021, https://www.newscientist.com/lastword/mg24933241-300-how-long-is-now-the-gap-between-the-past-and-future-continued/.

partner as well. My friends, colleagues, and family often refer to me as the "soulful one" because I very, very rarely do anything that doesn't feed my soul—well, maybe with the exception of paying taxes.

So how do you actually find your True North and tap into spirit? Once we have the clearing of mind, body, and heart (that we spent time doing in Part 1 of the book) we need in order for the soul to shine—and for us to be able to really distinguish that from the mind chattering or the body aching or the heart wanting—it really comes down to that gut feeling one has. And the best way I know to really be able to connect with that is through meditation. Getting aligned with your energy and stepping outside of your thoughts. Nature can also help you get there. So can soulful conversations with your tribe.

I gave myself the gift of Transcendental Meditation for my birthday in 2015 and was trained over three days. The following year I did a silent weekend meditation with Buddhist monks in San Francisco. I've done walking meditations, silent hiking meditations, swimming meditations. Some people find the meditation that works for them and stick with it. Mine has been a mashup of the various methods and that seems to work for me. The beauty of meditation is that it compounds, so your ability to step into awareness is much faster and deeper with practice.

Repetition is important. It's not like one day you look up and find your True North. It's in the self- and soul-discovery that you get pointed that way more and more. I still continue to reorient myself. True North isn't a destination. It's a compass. It's a beacon. It's a way of walking through life. I think that there should be time and space allowed to discover one's soul and meditate and all that, but spirituality should really be actionable. It's in everything you do and how you live your life.

So, what if you've cleared your mind, you've cleared your heart, your body's not aching, but you're feeling resistant to meditating? I recommend taking a look at what that resistance is about. If sitting down and meditating feels like too much, figure out what else you can do to get into a zone in which the mind isn't dominating. You could try another kind of meditation: walking meditation, lying-down meditation, swimming meditation, dancing meditation, you name it. I would suggest starting with a moving meditation. Or playing. Play is so valuable here because it helps you get into the zone or a state of flow. It's outside your daily activities—you're not making a checklist or going through a to-do list or problem solving everything that's on your mind.

From what I've experienced, people often find themselves resistant to meditation either because they have a hard time sitting still—which is why I recommend the other meditation styles—or because they think of it as a waste of time since they're not "doing" anything. But it's this "not doing and just being" that is the essence of mindfulness, spirituality, and awareness. Sylvia Boorstein, a founding teacher of Spirit Rock, coined the phrase "Don't just do something, sit there," which is funny and very true. It of course doesn't mean that we never do anything, but that we make time to be still and present before we do.

Please note that meditation can sometimes trigger past traumas. If you do find yourself triggered mentally and in deep emotional pain as a result of meditation, please stop and resolve with a mental health professional before approaching again. Meditation can sometimes open old wounds, and if big enough, one can get negatively affected by them without proper support. It's a very fine line, as meditation can also help release the past. Meditation is a choice. So please trust your intuition. If it's uncomfortable because you have not done it before, then please give it some time. If it is bringing up very strong emotions and affecting your mind severely, please stop and consult a mental health professional. Do not go it alone.

With both play and meditation, you're stepping outside of the way you think in order to gain awareness. That truly is the definition of awakening: to be able to see yourself in life, in the universe, doing what you do and realizing that everything you do is a part of a greater whole.

You'll recognize that you're on track when you feel that sense of connectedness and being a part of something greater than yourself. It's something that you feel, not just something conceptual. Your mind might feel like it's floating rather than trying to process something. You'll notice that you're in a certain flow, that there is energy moving through you, that you're present and grounded in the moment.

Funny enough, these days the times when I am most aware of my True North are when I am off track and realize I am not on course. It's usually when I feel ungrounded, overwhelmed, or something feels off. Sometimes I'm not even aware that I'm feeling off until I catch myself. Once I do, I stop whatever I am doing—or finish what I am doing as soon as possible—and either go for a walk, meditate, or call someone in my tribe to process with. Oftentimes, I walk and talk with my wife, which is grounding, or if I feel I need alone time, I ask for it and head out into nature. Water is a huge calming and grounding resource for me, and luckily we live very close to the ocean. I've often meditated to the ebb and flow of waves...or closed my eyes and just listened to the sounds of the ocean, the seagulls, and the breeze. And then I am back in my flow. Hopefully the following exercises will help you find yours.

## AWAKENING COMPASSION

When you get comfortable with meditating regularly and ready for an even deeper connection with your soul and the souls of others, you may want to practice a type of meditation called Tonglen. Think of it as spiritual giving. It is one of the most powerful spiritual practices we can do. Tonglen is basically the meditative practice of breathing in all that is not well in the world and breathing out loving kindness, acceptance, forgiveness, and compassion. I'm sure right about now you're wondering why the hell anyone would do such a thing given the existing challenges and pains of our daily lives. Why would someone act as a filter for all the crap that is out there in our world and offer relief and love in return? Isn't that the work of the Mother Theresas, Popes, and Dalai Lamas of our world? Yes and no. Yes, in that it is exactly this generosity of spirit that makes the Dalai Lamas of our world so powerful, but also no because it is something that we can (and in my not-so-humble opinion) should, actively practice as global citizens.

The practice of Tonglen began in the eleventh century when leprosy had devastated Tibet. The practice was brought over from India by meditation masters in order to help those who were suffering in order to heal themselves and in return heal others, gifting the practice forward to others in need. The word Tonglen is the combination of two Tibetan terms: "tong," which means "letting go" and "len," which means accepting.

Global citizenship and goodwill aside, the practice of Tonglen also helps to reverse our very human tendency to avoid suffering and seek pleasure. You can practice Tonglen as part of your meditation when you are moved to do so or when in the presence of someone who is mourning, ill, in pain, or suffering in any way. With each breath in, we are accepting the suffering of the person/group/community/country/world, and with every breath out, we are offering relief and compassion. Breathe in for all of us, and breathe out for all of us. Receiving and sending. Taking and giving.

Tonglen can be practiced on the spot any time you encounter anything distressing or unwelcome in your life, whether it be a war in another part of the world, an injustice, or a family member who is ill.

Tonglen is active compassion. It gives us a sense of connection to others, it awakens the spirit of giving within us, and reverses our tendency to self-focus. And the more you do it, the stronger it becomes. Give it a try when you feel ready to do so. The meditation is in four stages:

1. Sit comfortably, close your eyes, and relax your body, focusing on your breath as you inhale and exhale. (Note: If you are new to meditation, the Day One exercise of this chapter walks you through a guided meditation. You're welcome

to review and practice it before attempting Tonglen.)

2.  Now link intention to your breath. Begin visualizing the experience that is creating the suffering and allow the feeling that arises with it. Imagine lifting the pain, the sadness, the grief, the angst, the confusion, the anger, and the despair from another person with each breath in.

3.  On the exhale, breathe out light, love, peace, and kindness. You are in harmony with the darkness you inhale and the light you exhale, the suffering you inhale and the relief you exhale.

4.  Now imagine others in similar situations who you may or may not know. Breathe in their suffering and offer them solace. That is the power of Tonglen.

Once you feel complete, go back to concentrating on your breath without the visualization, and when ready, open your eyes and slowly return to the room or space where you are.

# Week 5

## The Daily Purge

Have you been continuing your Daily Purge? If you tried out a different way of purging last week, or a different time of day, how did it go? Do you want to continue with that this week or try something else? I encourage you to use this week for any final experimenting. Next week you can settle into the Daily Purge method most likely to become a habit for you, and hopefully you'll continue it well after finishing this book.

# Week 5

## Exercise: Reclaiming Your Soul

As a reminder, these weekly exercises are here to help this book become experiential for you—so you aren't just reading the book and thinking, "That's a nice concept" and putting it down, but living it. Hopefully by this point in your journey, you've bookmarked at least a handful that you might return to in the future.

**Day One:**   Try a guided meditation for ten minutes. Meditation is the beeline to everything else when it comes to the soul, so I encourage you not to bypass this exercise! If you have a hard time sitting down to meditate, try another approach, like a walking meditation. There are many guided meditations that you can find online. Here's a guided meditation for breath, which is an excellent place to start.

Place one hand on your stomach and the other on your chest. Feel your chest rise and fall. Now feel your stomach rise and fall. Inhale through your nostrils... and exhale through your mouth. There is only the breath. Nothing else to think about but your breath. Concentrate on it. When other thoughts enter, thank them gently, let them go, and return to concentrating on your breath.

Inhale to the count of four, hold for three counts, and exhale to the count of five.

So, inhale...two, three, four. Hold...two, three. Exhale... two, three, four, five.

Inhale...two, three, four. Hold...two, three. Exhale... two, three, four, five.

Inhale...two, three, four. Hold...two, three. Exhale... two, three, four, five.

Now focus on how the breath is entering and moving through your nostrils.

Inhale...two, three, four. Hold...two, three. Exhale... two, three, four, five.

Notice your breath as it passes slowly through your nasal passages, and down your throat.

Inhale...two, three, four. Hold...two, three. Exhale... two, three, four, five.

Feel your breath fill your lungs.

Inhale...two, three, four. Hold...two, three. Exhale... two, three, four, five.

Feel how your lungs expand and then relax and expand again.

Inhale...two, three, four. Hold...two, three. Exhale... two, three, four, five.

As the air travels down your lungs and out again, ease into it and relax.

Inhale...two, three, four. Hold...two, three. Exhale... two, three, four, five.

All there is this moment, this breath.

Inhale...two, three, four. Hold...two, three. Exhale... two, three, four, five.

All there is this moment, this breath.

Inhale...two, three, four. Hold...two, three. Exhale... two, three, four, five.

How does your breath feel as it exits through your mouth? How does it feel on your lips?

Inhale...two, three, four. Hold...two, three. Exhale... two, three, four, five.

Imagine your breath as a wave of love, entering through your nostrils, traveling down your throat, expanding in your lungs, and relaxing into you before traveling back up your lungs, through your throat, and out of your mouth.

Inhale love...two, three, four. Hold love...two, three. Exhale love...two, three, four, five.

Inhale love...two, three, four. Hold love...two, three. Exhale love...two, three, four, five.

Inhale love...two, three, four. Hold love...two, three. Exhale love...two, three, four, five.

Continue this for at least ten minutes and no more than twenty minutes. When you're ready to stop the meditation, inhale, hold, and count backwards from five, four, three, two, one.

Your breathing meditation is now complete.

**Day Two:** Walk in solitude in nature for at least ten minutes. Whatever nature you can get to, whether that is a nearby park or backyard or stream or a local mountain range.

**Day Three:** Today's exercise is a day-long observation exercise. If you are interacting with people throughout the day, observe those interactions. Notice where you believe there's spirit and where it's missing. (For instance, if you recognize the giddy excitement of your kids as you help them get dressed for school, or if you go to work and experience the sternness and exhaustion of your boss.) If you are spending your day solo, observe what media you're consuming. Notice where it fulfills your heart, where it just fills the space and if it contracts your heart.

Over the course of the day, pay attention to which interactions and engagements feed your soul and which detract from it or contract it.

**Day Four:**    For the entire morning of day four, set an intention to live and interact with the world from a soul space rather than an ego space. Step into a space of awareness so that your ego isn't at play and interact from the soul.

In the afternoon, let go of that intention.

And in the evening, reflect on your experience. What did you notice? What do you want to take with you?

**Day Five:**    Think of an area of conflict in your life that could use your soul's attention. (Perhaps a relationship with a relative or colleague.) Now meditate on it for ten minutes—let yourself sit with the possibility of how that relationship could look different if you approached it from soul space. If you feel moved to do so, journal about it or draw what arises.

**Day Six:**    Play with your soul. Today, let your soul be your playmate and go have a good time together.

**Day Seven:**    Commit to something that is soulful that you will do for yourself repeatedly.

It could be something just for you—say, birdwatching for ten minutes a day—or it could be larger, perhaps something in your community. Decide what you are committing to, then make it a formal commitment by either saying the words aloud or writing them down and signing your name.

This is officially the end of Week 5...and what a week it has been! Does your soul feel omnipresent? I hope so. Mine is here to stay and I have easy access to it—all the time! I wake up with it, play with it, create with it, and sleep with it. It is with me 24/7. It doesn't mean that I don't get upset, that I walk around in a zen state, that I always say and do the right thing. What it means is that everything—and I mean literally everything—I do in my life generates from it, or I don't do it. This is how I know I am living my life's purpose. I hope I have helped clear the way for you too. So, what's next? Well, that is up to you...

# Week 6

## (Re)Write Your Story

> "You're under no obligation to be the same person you were five minutes ago."
>
> **—Alan Watts**

I have a distinct memory of driving home from work shortly after the breakup. It was winter and it got dark out early. It was also cold and wet. I had some sort of soul-steering music on. All very dramatic. I was thinking that I didn't want to just write a new chapter of my life—I wanted an entirely new book! I thought, *What if you're able to create a life that would be unrecognizable to the person you are right now? What would that life look like? Who would be in it? Who and what would be left behind in the book you're about to finish? What will you be doing? How will you be spending your days? Where would you be living? Where would you travel to? How will you contribute to the world?*

I realize that not everyone has the privilege of rewriting their story so completely, but we always have a choice to be different. Lasting change is very, very rarely accomplished overnight, but taking steps toward a new direction is instantaneous. These steps repeated create new habits and little habits repeated turn into my new way of living. As mentioned in the last chapter, I have gotten so in the habit of living a mindful life that the only time I am aware that I am not being "aware" is when I am thrown off-course. When that happens, I quickly do whatever is in my capacity to become realigned.

## STRIPPING AWAY ALL THAT IS NOT YOU

One of my all-time favorite films is *The Black Stallion*. It's an amazing film all around, but the final scene is powerful. Not sure if you've seen it, but a young boy washes up on a deserted island with a gorgeous Arabian stallion after a shipwreck. They soon become friends and the horse finally allows the boy to ride bareback and they have many amazing rides in the sun—just the two of them.

Then they're found and the boy gets to keep the horse. He starts training as a jockey, and he enters a major race. In the race, he and his horse have a bad start out of the gate and begin falling behind. At some point, the boy does the very thing I want to highlight in this chapter. He starts stripping away his goggles, his helmet, his whip, and every-thing that he's been taught and starts riding the horse the way he did on the island. As they do, they start gaining momentum and end up winning the race. An amazing visual example of what is possible when you shed all the "should dos" and trust your inner fire.

If you stripped away everything you've learned in your life—what you must study, the work you have to do, how productive you have to be in order to feel/look useful, the money you must have, the stuff you have to buy, and so on—and all the other crap that blocks us from truly celebrating ourselves as we truly are, what would remain? After five weeks of detoxing, playing, and finding your True North, it is time to rewrite the story of your life exactly as you would like to have it. This rewrite will act as your promise to yourself and your manifesto. You're welcome to amend it at any time.

## MANIFEST(O) LIKE YOU MEAN IT

> "Life isn't about finding yourself. Life is about creating yourself."
>
> **—George Bernard Shaw**

> "You don't become what you want, you become what you believe."
>
> **—Oprah Winfrey**

I cannot think about manifesting without thinking of Oprah. I recall an interview where she was asked if she considered herself a "manifester." She replied without hesitation that she was a "master manifester" (now she uses "powerful manifester" because the word "master" is getting such a bad rap), and she is truly a woman who walks her talk.

Oprah tells the story of how, for ten years, after every show she would shake hands and sign autographs—seven hundred people a day. Even though to her "it felt vapid, it felt meaningless." And then one day, she had to leave the studio early for a doctor's appointment, and she realized how much energy that post-show routine had been taking up, and she asked herself, "What do I want?" The answer was clear: "What I really want is to connect. I really want to know who these people are." So, after the next show, and for every show thereafter, she began talking to the audience instead of signing autographs. And what she learned from them guided the future direction of the show, as she discovered that her audience was searching for more meaning and struggling themselves with the question of "What do I want?"[101]

Here's what Oprah has to say about manifesting: "I have seen it happen over and over and over again, and I actually have come to know that this whole planetary experience, it's just like a classroom. And you control a lot by your thoughts, and we control a lot by our joined thoughts, by what I believe, and what you believe, and we come together as a community and we believe, and then that's what shows up for us. That's why we have the government that we do, that's why we have elected officials that we do, the schools, and the world that we have. So, when I started to figure that out for myself and understand how

---

101 Oprah Winfrey, "Oprah on manifesting what you want," interviewed by Jeff Weiner, LinkedIn Studios,14:41, https://www.linkedin.com/learning/influencer-interview-oprah-winfrey/oprah-on-manifesting-what-you-want.

powerful a manifester I was, I, actually, it made me more consciously aware of, to be careful of what I think and what I ask for."[102]

This is an important lesson. If "manifestation is bringing something tangible into your life through attraction and belief,"[103] as the *Oprah Daily* website declares, then it matters what you are trying to attract. I joke that I've always gotten what I've wanted, but never on my timeline. And it's so true. I think that's how manifesting works. As long as you're trying to control it, it won't happen. So, it kind of feels like a dichotomy, but it's not, because you're trying. You're working as hard as hell to intend it, and yet, you're not supposed to control it. I think that *is* the trick, in that you can't have an attachment to the outcome.

So, what's the process? How do you manifest? There are four main steps: getting very clear about what it is that you want; stating it—putting it out there; working as hard as hell to move toward it; and letting go of the outcome. That's it. That's the process.

Within that, there are a couple of other elements that will help. The first is gratitude. Being appreciative and thankful for what you receive. A gratitude journal is a nice tool for this. So is a blessing at mealtimes, or simply pausing in appreciation when you step outside each day.

The second element is letting go of your resistance and your limiting beliefs. (Some of the exercises in the earlier chapters may help you with this.) As Oprah says, "Telling yourself you're not good enough, you're not

---

102  Ibid.
103  Kimberly Zapata, "How to Manifest Anything You Desire," Oprah Daily, July 22, 2022, https://www.oprahdaily.com/life/a30244004/how-to-manifest-anything/.

worthy enough, you're not smart enough, you're not enough—it's a tape that's playing for a lot of people.... If you're not conscious of that, then you end up acting out of that belief system and not what you know to be the truest or want to be the truest for yourself. You don't become what you want because so much of wanting is about living in the space of what you don't have."[104] It matters what energy you are putting out in the world. Oprah again: "The energy we put out in the world is the energy we get back.... If you want more love in your life, set your intention to be more loving. If you seek kindness, focus your energy on empathy and compassion."[105]

I feel like I've manifested so many different things. My two kids being a fine example. (My ex didn't want to have kids. That changed as soon as they arrived in our lives, but it made getting there kind of an uphill battle for me.) I was really clear from the time I was twelve years old that I wanted to have kids. I really didn't care how, and I didn't care where they came from. I just wanted to be a mom. And I also knew that I wanted a boy and a girl.

The adoption process was not easy, especially for Kian, my first, the boy. And I just knew that it would happen. I remember having set his baby room up far before we knew who he was. I could see the crib from our bed. I would just look into that crib and think, "There will be a baby in there soon. There will be a baby in there soon." Sure enough, there was a baby in there soon. Though not soon enough because his adoption took three years. And Iman's took two years, though it was certainly a lot smoother all around. The first adoption was not easy. I

104  Ibid.
105  Ibid.

lost two referrals in Azerbaijan, then went to Kazakhstan. Nothing happened there. Then went to Guatemala and lost one referral there before Kian came along. It was a three-year process. Very long, very painful. But I just knew that it would happen, and it did.

Another example is that after the breakup, even through my grief, I was absolutely clear that I would have a new partner. I remember reading something that said part of the manifesting is really feeling what it feels like. If I'm manifesting having a child, feeling what it really feels like to be holding that child. Not just looking at the crib and imagining it, but *feeling* it. If you were 100 percent sure that what you wanted, you would have, what would that feel like?

So, I remember standing on the balcony of my home and really embodying what it would feel like to have a new life partner and to be in love and happy and have it be committed, stable, and steady. Which sounds great—but quite difficult when you're in a lot of pain—to have that clearing and have it feel authentic. That was the first time I did it. And then I would repeat that, just like, *yes, this is just a matter of time before I feel this way.* And sure enough, it was. It did take a few trials. I dated a few people before Tracey came along. But I was positive. I was positive that it would happen. I knew what it felt like. It was in the repetition and moving forward toward it, even though I had no idea who the target was. It was sort of like the babies—I didn't know what the baby would look like. I just knew what the outcome was. I knew what motherhood could feel like. I knew what being partnered could feel like. And I kept returning to that thought and feeling.

A third manifestation is that I started the world's first 24/7 LGBTQIA channel dedicated to queer women (trans and non-binary inclusive). I started it as a website in 2009, purely with the desire and the intention that there should be a place where you get good quality lesbian content (that was not pornographic) online. I started the website, not knowing much about building websites at that time, but knowing it should be there and setting it forth, working as hard as heck to make it happen, and letting go of set outcomes, and watching it grow. And it's happened, which is a beautiful thing. Over the years it's grown to have a reach of over 250 million devices and households, a dedicated staff, and a great social following. Our YouTube channel[106] (as of this writing) has more than 560 million views, 14 million hours watched, and 909,000 subscribers...and is still growing rapidly.

So, get clear about what you want. Put that intention out into the world. Work toward it. And then let go of the outcome, and trust the process. You'll be rewriting your story and creating a personal manifesto in this week's exercises, and that should start your process of clarity.

## FINDING YOUR *RAISON D'ÊTRE*

"You must become the producer, director and actor in the unfolding story of your life."

**—Wayne Dyer**

---

106  OML Television, accessed November 22, 2022, https://www.youtube.com/omltelevision.

If you've done any soul searching before reading this book, you've probably run across books, articles, and blog posts that talk about following your bliss. "Following your bliss" sounds great, but in my opinion it is a form of spiritual bypassing and spiritual window shopping, since a "blissful" life is a fantasy. A "mindful" life, yes. A "woke" life, yes. A "blissful" life is the stuff of Instagram posts and #livingmybestlife selfies.

Raison d'être is a French term that means "reason for being." Reason for *being*, not "reason for *doing*." One of the things that has always fascinated and frustrated me about Western culture, especially in the United States, is that people define themselves by what they do. You ask someone, "Who are you?" and they'll respond with "I'm a banker," or an engineer, a plumber, a marketer, and so on. So, who are they when they're not banking, engineering, plumbing, or marketing, do they stop being?

We are drilled from an early age to think that way. Even at a young age, we're taught to identify ourselves as a student, not just a kid or little human. One of the biggest issues with defining ourselves by what we do is that, with such a goal-specific mentality, we often feel empty when we're not working. We also tend to compare ourselves to others who are doing the same things better or faster. I am by no means suggesting you give up what you do, or devaluing it. What I am suggesting is that our raison d'être is much wider and deeper than what we do. And unless we examine the different aspects of ourselves and what is at the center of it, we will forever be searching for that ephemeral "blissful" life.

# IKIGAI

> "Our ikigai is different for all of us, but one thing we have in common is that we are all searching for meaning."
>
> **—Héctor García Puigcerver, *Ikigai: The Japanese Secret to a Long and Happy Life***

Ikigai (yes, pronounced eeky-guy, but nothing eeky or male specific about it. ;) ) is the Japanese term for one's reason for being or raison d'être. It is made from two Japanese words: iki, meaning "life," and gai, meaning "effect, result, worth or benefit." What's particularly great about ikigai is that it is not just a philosophical theory or a concept that you can discuss over coffee or meditate on. It isn't a woo-woo spiritual leader instructing you to trust your intuition without any actual guidance, or saying, "Yeah, leave your wife and kids and go fishing on some island and follow your bliss." It's a practical guide to following your passion that integrates the other essential elements. Ikigai is the *What Color is Your Parachute?* for a rich, soulful life. There is actually a formula for ikigai—a Venn diagram, to be exact.

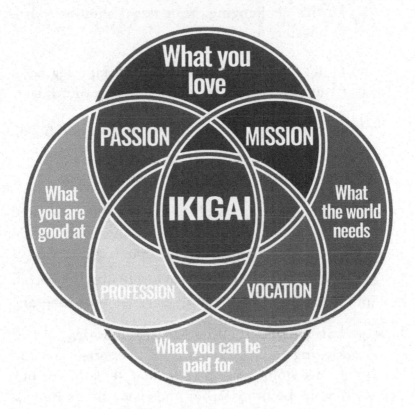

As the website Savvy Tokyo explains, "[a] combination of the Japanese words 'iki' (生き), which translates to 'life,' and 'gai' (甲斐), which is used to describe value or worth, ikigai is all about finding joy in life through purpose. In other words, your ikigai is what gets you up every morning and keeps you going."[107]

Here are a few aspects that reinforce how ikigai is distinct from simply following your bliss:

107 Lucy Dayman, "Ikigai: The Japanese Concept of Finding Purpose in Life," Savvy Tokyo, January 15, 2020, https://savvytokyo.com/iki-gai-japanese-concept-finding-purpose-life/.

- "It's challenging. Your ikigai should lead to mastery and growth.

- It's your choice. You feel a certain degree of autonomy and freedom pursuing your ikigai.

- It involves a commitment of time and belief, perhaps to a particular cause, skill, trade, or group of people.

- It boosts your well-being. Ikigai is associated with positive relationships and good health. It gives you more energy than it takes away."[108]

So, let's dive into the nitty gritty of ikigai with an example, spelling out each element of that Venn diagram.

- **What you love.** Whether it's painting or it's designing homes or it's playing sports, what do you love doing? Put that in that section. For our example, both my father and sister are architects, so we'll use "designing homes."

- **What the world needs.** What do you feel that the world needs that can go along with what you love? If you love designing homes, the world needs homes. People in the world need homes, and that's what to put in that section.

---

108  Melody Wilding, "The Japanese Concept 'Ikigai" is a Formula for Happiness and Meaning," *Better Humans*, November 30, 2017, https://betterhumans.pub/the-japanese-concept-ikigai-is-a-formula-for-happiness-and-meaning-8e497e5afa99.

- **What you can get paid for.** Where are you now in relation to what you've just identified? If you're getting paid for it now, put that down. If not, what is that thing, and what are the next steps to get there? For our example, maybe you could be an architect or an interior designer. Architects and interior designers both get paid for different aspects of designing homes. Then, if you want to design homes and become an architect or an interior designer, and what you're doing right now is working at a coffee shop, what are the steps you need to take in order to get paid for what you love doing? Probably, your next steps require getting a degree and finding internships, moving in that direction.

- **What you're good at.** What are you good at? Whether it is something you're naturally good at or what you've become good at, put that down. Often what you're good at goes along with what you love, though not always. For our example, maybe you're good with design, but you're not the best freeform designer with your hands, as you're better with a computer. So, interior design might not be the best fit, but you think that you could rock it with CAD (computer-aided design) software, and therefore make a great architect.

The intersection of what you love and what you're good at is passion: *I'm passionate about designing homes using CAD.* The intersection between what you love and what the world needs is mission: *I love designing homes and want to do so for anyone who needs a home.* The intersection between what the world needs and what you can get paid for is vocation: *Once I get my architectural degree, I'm going to build homes that are incredibly eco-friendly, there's a need for that.* The intersection between what you can get paid for and what you're good at is profession: *I'm going to be an architect.* And that's how you find your ikigai.

In my own life, *what I love* is what I'm doing in this book—being in the conversation of the greater transformation of people and our world. *What the world needs* is exactly that—that we have a greater collective understanding and conversations about how we can evolve individually and, therefore, collectively. That the individual self-transformation will ultimately result in a world transformation if there's enough of us doing it. It's sort of like herd transformation. *What I can get paid for hopefully in the future will be speaking engagements and such, but right now, what I get paid for* is what my vocation has been, which is in the realm of marketing, advertising, video and film production, and television. What I've been trying to do in the past few years and am doing with this book, frankly, is bridging that gap to move closer to what I want to be doing. And *what I'm really good at* is authenticity, bringing authenticity out in others, and creating connections that are very real, honest, and human. If by the time I'm done doing what I'm doing on this earth, I've been able to create a more humane humanity, I'm happy. So that's how I know that I'm living my ikigai.

If I'm able to create a more humane humanity, that's me living my ikigai. It's the constant mindfulness of my own life and working toward my contribution to the world.

I think that it's very hard to find your purpose and not have that somehow have a positive impact on the world, because true intention is a soul intention, it's not an ego intention. In that the ego may say, "Well, I want to own the next Enron and make a bunch of money and I don't care who I screw over," but that's not true intention, that's ego driven. True intention is the soul-driven intention, and soul-driven intention manifested benefits the world. Now imagine a world where people are honoring and following their soul-driven intention. If that feels too lofty, imagine your loved ones or your community doing so.

> "Let us remember: One book, one pen, one child, and one teacher can change the world."
>
> **—Malala Yousafzai**

To discover your own ikigai, start with the Venn diagram questions. Map it out, see if it feels right, give it a try. Because I do think it's not a one-time thing. I think that it takes time to really feel it out. And I think that it also evolves, even though it's the same direction.

When I was twelve, I got really interested in acting. Had I known back then that public speaking was an option, I may have picked that instead, but it's all been about the same thing. It's all been about being in conversation and speaking with people—and growth, participating, human connection, and so on. So, my ikigai took some time to be discovered, but it hasn't ever really changed. That center hasn't really changed. It's all the stuff around it that has changed and is now becoming more solidified.

You're not going to be creating an entirely different ikigai in five or ten years. That centerpiece will remain the same. But the other parts of your ikigai Venn diagram may change depending on how you evolve. That's the journey. That's the process.

> "The happiest people are not the ones who achieve the most. They are the ones who spend more time than others in a state of flow."
>
> —Héctor García Puigcerver, *Ikigai: The Japanese Secret to a Long and Happy Life*

## IF YOU FALTER, BEGIN AGAIN

I took a workshop with Barbara De Angelis a few years after my big separation. I had been dating a woman for two years and had broken up with her and was feeling like a failure. Not like a total failure, just "Okay, Well, that one didn't work." It was a rebound and I knew it. And I had an aha moment when Barbara De Angelis talked about how we can begin again. That at any given point we can begin again. Like the Alan Watts quote at the top of the chapter, we're not obligated to be who we were yesterday or even five minutes ago.

I think that the more mindful we are, and the more present that we are, the easier it is to begin again. As humans, we are rarely present. We flip flop between the past and the future. This is pretty much the human condition—reminiscing or regretting the past or making up scenarios about the future. But the more we live a mindful life—which is a more present life—the more we realize that we're not our past and we're just fantasizing about our future. So, it's much easier to begin again.

Being in the workshop with Barbara De Angelis, I really got that. The story I was telling myself, *"Yes, I just got out of another relationship. It only lasted two years. Yet again, I failed,"* was a story based on the past—and I was no longer that person. I could easily be a clear slate. And that's what I decided to do at that workshop, and what I've continued to do. To say to myself, *"Okay, begin again."* And begin again. And begin again. And begin again.

You can literally say this every morning: "All right, well this didn't work, begin again." Unless you don't want to begin again, then, "continue on." But at any given point you truly can begin again, regardless of your age. My friend Gina Pell coined the term "Perennials," to describe people who are forever growing, forever curious. Somebody who's in their twenties may think that it's easy to begin, and somebody who's in their sixties may not feel that way, but that's not the truth. You really can, regardless of your circumstances. And to whatever extent it is possible for you. You may not be able to see the road ahead, but you can take the next step and the next step and the next.

> "The journey of a thousand miles begins with one step."
>
> —Lao Tzu

Beginning again is the refinement of ikigai. Going back to our aspiring architect from the previous section: you work your ass off, you get that degree, you're in an architectural company that you've tried really hard to get into, and then you have an asshole of a boss and because of that, you get fired, and you feel like the biggest failure ever, because you *had* that dream, you had what it was. But you can begin again. As long as you're moving toward the direction of your ikigai, you're good. It's a bump in the road.

And bumps in the road are going to happen. It could be that you're moving in the direction of your ikigai and you lose a loved one, or you get really sick. It shouldn't alter your ikigai. Begin again.

Ikigai becomes your manifesto, frankly. That regardless of what happens, you get back on track. That's your True North...and you keep walking in that direction—no matter what!

## DON'T FALL INTO A SPIRITUAL COMA

Having been around the spiritual block, so to speak, a few times, I am incredibly aware of its loopholes and faults. Spirituality on its own is mind-blowing, spectacular, jaw-dropping, and magical. What we humans do with it is what creates the issues. We follow people blindly thinking they have the answers. We take a few workshops and think we've mastered ourselves. We hold transformational figures to such high standards that they are bound to disappoint at some point—because at the end of the day, week, month, year...we are all just human. Do I believe that there are many different levels of consciousness in this world? Absolutely. Do I believe there are incredible teachers that we can learn from? Definitely. Do I believe anyone has all the answers? Definitely not. Would I follow one teacher and discount others? Absolutely not.

As mentioned earlier in the book, one of the reasons I am drawn to Buddhism is that it is technically not a religion. There is no outer God to pray to or seek. *All* the work is internal. The deeper in you go, the greater your consciousness. And there is no destination. There are no heavens or hells...except within ourselves and what we (humans) create. This is not unique to Buddhism. There are now many spiritual teachers and many paths. It is up to you to choose them. Combine them, deep dive into them, walk away from them, walk back to them. This journey is yours and yours alone.

The world is not rosy. It never was and never will be. Why? I don't know. But I do believe we're here to learn, evolve, and transform. Where do our souls come from when we're born and where they go after we die is still anyone's guess. Isn't that fascinating? With all our research, brilliant minds, countless universities, all the technology in the world, we still have no idea. Not a clue! I don't find that depressing. To me, it's the universe asking us to stay curious. To explore more and opine less.

# Week 6

## The Daily Purge

By this time, The Daily Purge should be a given—a habit. It's become so habitual for me that it is no different than brushing my teeth or combing my hair. Six minutes of releasing the toxic thoughts and feelings that are holding you down. Start now. Tell them to get out, show them the door, push them out, scream them out, doodle them out, dance, walk, or swim them out. Just do so with intention. Purge, purge, purge!!

# Week 6

Exercise: Design Your New Life

**Day One:**   Much like the Daily Purge, without over-thinking it, write down all the things you no longer want in your life. This doesn't mean you have to take action on them, or even do anything about them, but jot them down and write about why you want to let go of them. Do this for at least ten minutes and no more than thirty minutes. Don't pay attention to your grammar or spelling or worry that someone will see it. Just write. What you include could be as big as "I no longer want to live in this town" or "I no longer want so and so in my life" to as mundane as "I no longer want to wear those shoes, they always hurt my feet." Whatever you don't want, leave it here.

**Day Two:**   Now that you've stated everything you don't want, for the next ten to thirty minutes, without stopping, write down everything you want from this moment to the rest of your life. It doesn't matter if you don't know what you want in thirty years or you have no idea what your career trajectory is. It doesn't matter if you believe it will or will not happen. Just write what comes, without overthinking it. It can be as spectacular or mundane as you'd like. Please note that while you can write outlandish possibilities like, "I want to live on Pluto," or "I want to breathe underwater," or "I want to live in this body forever," those are going to dilute what is truly possible for you to manifest in this lifetime.

**Day Three:**  Get a big piece of paper and draw out everything you wrote on Day One. It doesn't matter how well you can draw. Include everything and everyone mentioned on Day One. Take a long look at it and say goodbye to each part: "Goodbye, nitpicking my husband," "Goodbye, always second-guessing myself," "Goodbye, mean boss," "Goodbye, job I can't stand," and so on. Now find a very safe place to burn the drawing. Watch it burn while saying, "Thank you. You are no longer needed."

**Day Four:**  Get a big piece of paper and draw your vision board from everything you wrote on

Day Two. Be sure to have fun with it. You can make it as colorful as you like. Again, this is freeform, so it isn't about how well you draw, and it isn't for anyone else to see. This is a visual representation of everything you want in your life. It can serve as a basis for a more elaborate vision board later, if you'd like, but right now this exercise is about designing your life exactly as you would like it. It can look busy or it can look sparse. There is no right or wrong way to draw. Just make sure that every single thing you mentioned in Day Two is included.

**Day Five:**    Reach out to a trusted friend—one from your tribe—and present your vision board to them. This should be a non-judgmental friend who gets you and all your weirdness/quirks and loves you more for it. You can giggle at your doodles and scribbles, but tell them what you see. What's important is that you say it out loud, so the vision and manifesto aren't just in your head. Your friend is allowed to ask for clarification, but they cannot comment or critique. This is very important. They are there simply to receive and accept. (If for some reason you absolutely can't do this exercise with a trusted friend, please present your vision board while looking into a mirror and make an audio or video recording of your presentation.) Let your friend know there will be a follow up request, and you will tell them what it is the next day.

**Day Six:** Ask your friend to present back to you what you presented to them yesterday. (If you're reading ahead: please do not mention this to your friend when you are presenting to them, as you want them to stay present to what you are presenting and not worry about what they will or will not remember. This is important.) Much like yesterday, you can ask questions or for clarifications, but you cannot correct your friend or criticize. If you taped yourself instead of sharing with a friend, play back the recording.

This exercise is the most important exercise of the week because it will give you a glimpse of what you are manifesting in the world. We are, of course, all very human, so your friend may have misunderstood something, but having your vision mirrored back to you is highly insightful. If it is to your liking, you are set. If you see that a part of your vision is still blurry, spend time refining it. There is absolutely no right or wrong here. This is your song, your masterpiece, your book, your manifesto— what you leave in or out is completely up to you.

**Day Seven:** Create a short phrase or a word that will remind you of the commitment you have made to yourself. You can make up the word or have it be a mashup like iuhbkass or lovisdo. Repeat it to yourself enough times that you won't forget it, and let that word become your cue. So, the next time you hear that word—every time you hear that word—you know your ikigai, you know your True North, you know your manifesto. And you can repeat that word or that phrase at any moment to bring it all back.

We've come to the end of Week 6 and the process...and the book. If this is your first venture into the world of self-transformation, please view this book as a first step, a primer. If this is one of many self-transformation books you have read, I hope I have been of help to you on your journey. The important thing to remember—as cliche as it sounds—is that spirituality is a process and a life-long journey, not a destination. It is often messy, painful, uncomfortable, dark, and scary. It is also glorious, magical, healing, and infinite.

> "Once you know who you really are, being is enough. You feel neither superior to anyone nor inferior to anyone and you have no need for approval because you've awakened to your own infinite worth."
>
> **—Deepak Chopra**

# Acknowledgments

First and foremost, I want to thank my lovely wife, Tracey Mason, for showing me what real love, dedication, and commitment looks and feels like. You are my eternal charmer, perfect collaborator, partner in crime, playmate, soulmate, and laughmate (it's a word). I love you endlessly!

I want to thank my amazing son and daughter, Kian and Iman Etessam. The fact that I have two gorgeous souls who call me Maman everyday fills me with eternal joy.

To my sister, Lili Etessam (the boss), whose commitment to me and our family has always been immutable.

To my BFFs Mariah Hanson and Layli Shirani. Thank you for holding me up time and again when I have crumbled. Thank you for sitting with me in my deepest vulnerability and calling me on actions that have not served me. You have taught me the power of true friendship.

To my soul brother, Mehdi Anvarian, for keeping me real and grounded.

To Michelle Enlow and Tracey Broadman for showing up out of the blue when I needed it most and never leaving.

Last but not least, a huge thank you to my dear close friends and extended family. I am forever grateful for you and the community I have.